WRITING
FROM A
LEGAL PERSPECTIVE

By
GEORGE D. GOPEN
Assistant Professor of English
Director of Writing Programs
Loyola University of Chicago

ST. PAUL, MINN.
WEST PUBLISHING CO.
1981

Library of Congress Cataloging in Publication Data

Gopen, George D
 Writing from a legal perspective.

 1. Legal composition. I. Title.
KF250.G66   808'.06634   80-27849

ISBN 0-8299-2123-0

Gopen Legal Perspec.Writing M.T.B.

1st Reprint—1986

For Jill

*

III

ABOUT THE AUTHOR

Dr. George D. Gopen received a J.D. from the Harvard Law School and a Ph.D. from the English Department of the Harvard Graduate School. He is Director of Writing Programs and a member of the English Department of Loyola University of Chicago, where he also supervises writing programs for the Law School. He has previously taught at Harvard University and at the University of Utah, and he is a legal writing consultant for law firms and businesses in the Chicago area.

*

PREFACE

This book owes its genesis to the energy and far-sightedness of Professor John Muller, now of the University of Minnesota. He was Director of Writing at the University of Utah in 1975 when I arrived to take up a position in the Department of English. He asked me to create an advanced composition course for pre-law students and allowed me funds from a Departmental grant to hold a national workshop on the subject.

Professor Muller and I invited to that workshop Constance Bordwell of the University of Oregon, Kathleen Cekanski of Notre Dame, John Louis of the University of Connecticut, Oliver Schroeder, Jr. of Case Western Reserve, and Richard Rieke of the University of Utah. In a series of strenuous meetings we discussed the theoretical and practical problems involved and were able to decide on a structure for the course. This book includes many of the materials I have developed for the course at Utah and, since 1978, at Loyola University of Chicago. I have adapted the book for use both on the undergraduate level and at law schools.

I would like to thank Charles W. Murdock, Dean of Loyola's School of Law, for offering the course in the Summer Session to incoming first-year students, which quickly multiplied the number of times these materials could be taught and, as a result, revised.

I owe a great debt to Nina S. Appel, Associate Dean of Loyola's School of Law, who with endless energy has supported new programs for improving writing at the law school level. Her encouragement has been invaluable to me.

I also thank John S. Shea, Chairman of Loyola's Department of English, for his cooperation in making this course available to our undergraduates. I could not wish for a better chairman or a finer colleague and friend.

I have been unusually fortunate in having had several excellent people, good lawyers and good friends all, teach this course under my supervision at Loyola. I wish to thank Joann Wasem, Susan

PREFACE

Bogart, Barry Spevack, JoAnne Gazarek Bloom, Diane Karp, and William Braithwaite, all of whom have been inspiring both as teachers and critics of these materials.

My thanks also go to Professor Allen Frantzen of Loyola's Department of English and Professor Peter Sterling of the Anatomy Department of the University of Pennsylvania for reading parts of the manuscript and making consistently perceptive comments and suggestions.

Ellen Postal and Cheryl Sporlein did uncommonly accurate and speedy work in typing the manuscript and were of great help in the editing process.

I send special thanks to the graduate students of the Anatomy Department of the University of Pennsylvania, who offered me the hospitality of their study quarters and the support of their friendship during the book's long gestation period. They are its god-parents.

I have not the words for what I owe to my wonderful wife and best critic, Jill Einstein, who often understands me and what I am trying to do better than I myself am able. She makes Philadelphia an exciting place to be on Sunday.

GEORGE D. GOPEN

Chicago, Illinois
December, 1980

SUMMARY OF CONTENTS

*

TABLE OF CONTENTS

TABLE OF CONTENTS

WRITING FROM A LEGAL PERSPECTIVE

Chapter I

LAWYERS AND LANGUAGE

A. THE LAWYER'S AUDIENCE

Writing clear and precise prose is a most difficult task even under ideal conditions, but the lawyer faces the worst of all conditions, a hostile audience. When doctors write patient reports, their audiences will spare no pains in trying to interpret the prose as the writer intended. Doctors can rely on their audiences to ease the burden of communication somewhat. When a lawyer writes, on the other hand, it is most often for an audience that will do its best to find the weaknesses in the prose, even perhaps to find ways of turning the words against their intended meaning. Senior partners will prod it to discover what someone else would say in opposition; judges will poke holes in it to see if the argument will stand up under attack; and opposing counsel will twist and turn it so that the words belie the thought that bred them.

All writers face the problem of discovering what to say and how to say it so that the reader will understand precisely what was meant; but lawyers must also consider how to say it so that no one can intentionally misconstrue their meaning. They must write aggressively and defensively at the same time, not an easy task; and they must be able to evaluate their product with an objective eye when it is finished.

1

Even the simplest, most seemingly straightforward statements are precariously subject to attack by someone who is accustomed to manipulating language. Consider the anecdote of the professor who berated the owner of a fish market for displaying a sign in the store window that read:

FRESH FISH SOLD HERE TODAY

Prof.:   My good fellow, why need you tell us the fish is "fresh"? We must assume you would not advertise stale goods. 'Tis superfluous.

Owner: Beg pardon, Sir.
[He removes "TODAY" from the sign, leaving "FISH SOLD HERE."]

Prof.:   Now, now, there's a good chap; what need you that word Certainly if you were selling your fish only yesterday or tomorrow or Thursday week, you would not display your sign today. Superfluous, once more.

Owner: Beg pardon, Sir.
[He removes "TODAY" from the sign, leaving "FISH SOLD HERE."]

Prof.:   Now, now, there's a good chap; what need you that word "here"? Would you put up the sign here and sell your wares elsewhere and not mention the fact? Superfluity in the extreme!

Owner: Beg pardon, Sir.
[He removes "HERE" from the sign, leaving "FISH SOLD."]

Prof.:   "Sold"? "Sold," my friend? What! Do you take us for simpletons, that we might think you would hand out the stuff gratis? Is this not a shop? Must you not earn your living, and if not by selling, how else? Insulting, as well as superfluous!

Owner: Beg pardon, Sir.
[He removes "SOLD" from the sign, leaving "FISH."]

Prof.:   "Fish"? The most superfluous of all. Anyone with eyes and a nose (phew!) can tell without your printing it up for us what it is you offer for sale.

Owner: Beg pardon, Sir.
         [He removes "FISH," thus removing the sign completely.]

Prof.:   Dear, dear, my mercantile friend. Why have you no sign
         in your window? Has no one ever convinced you of the
         power of advertisement?

In the struggle for accurate self-expression, you may often feel
like you have only the most obvious fish to sell. Despite his
unpleasant manner, Professor Stodge makes a good point or two.
The five words "FRESH FISH SOLD HERE TODAY" seem to
communicate little more than the two words "FISH SHOP," and
therefore the sign may justifiably be criticized on the grounds of
verbosity. The shop owner had not considered carefully enough
what it was he wanted to convey. Did he have a special kind of
fish there that day? Is his fish fresher than that at other shops?
Did he have a sale going? Is his service friendlier? Does he take
charge cards? These are things he might well have wished to
communicate to passers-by.

We should not, however, overlook the Professor's errors in judgment. Is his comment about "FRESH" totally justified? Does
not the word convey more than the simple idea of "not stale"?
The smell of fish in a fish store is often so pungent that
merchants would do well to have the word "fresh" somewhere
about, adding a positive association to an otherwise negative experience. What of "HERE" and "TODAY"? Do they not convey
a sense of urgency to the public, that it should seize the moment
and buy fish at this very place? Perhaps this merchant might
have produced a sign that would have done a better job of getting
his message across, but it is unlikely that he had no message to
convey, as the Professor implies. The Professor here is the
archetype of the hostile audience. Words, like fish, have a way of
slipping through our fingers if we are not extremely careful in
handling them. We understand this when we look back on our
own words after much time and realize how inadequately they
expressed our intentions. We suffer for it when someone else
points out the inadequacy. The hostile audience of the lawyer is
all too quick to proffer this service, and all they need do to cause
trouble is demonstrate that the lawyer's words do not compel the
interpretation the lawyer wishes. That the words could mean

what the lawyer wants does not adequately counterbalance their criticism.

EXERCISE

Choose to represent either the plaintiff or the defendant in the following hypothetical case, and write a 3-4 page argument for your side. Do no research. Consult no lawyers or friends. Record only your own thoughts. The purpose is not that you "get the right answer," but rather that you try to express opinions you already have as clearly and as forcibly as possible. Remember, you will be trying to convince someone who is not already in agreement with you. You must persuade them that your way of looking at the matter is the best way. Therefore do not merely label the issues; argue about them, explain them, and develop your thoughts to a logical conclusion.

Hypothetical: Sam Square vs. the Paris Cinema

On June 17 a half-page advertisement appeared in the city's leading newspaper:

WATCH FOR SALLY'S SEDUCTIVE SWINGERS

The ad included a large picture to three seductive-looking women, as scantily clad as a newspaper would allow. The ad ran daily for three weeks. On July 8 it was replaced by a picture of two dogs luridly gazing at one another in the foreground, while in the background a man and a woman gazed at each other in the same fashion over a backyard-type fence. The caption, in large letters read:

SIZZLE WITH THE SWAPPING SUBURBANITES

That ad ran for two weeks.

On July 22 it was replaced by the following ad, which appeared simultaneously on billboards, telephone poles, and in flyers which were distributed on street corners:

ANNOUNCING !!! The opening of the **PARIS CINEMA** !!!
OUR FIRST FEATURES
SALLY'S SEDUCTIVE SWINGERS
and
SWAPPING SUBURBANITES
All films rated **XXXX**   !   !   !   !   !   !
Special couples prices!
Convenient to downtown shopping!
Things you've never seen before!

People of all ages came to see the new theater and its attractions.

Samuel Square owns the store adjacent to the new cinema, a haberdashery shop catering to a distinctly conservative clientele ("A Square hat is a fair hat," "The Right People Think Square," and so forth). Sam finds his profits declining drastically as the theater grows in popularity. He hires a lawyer and sues the Paris Cinema for causing his loss of profits, for showing obscene films, and for corrupting the public.

B. THE LAWYER'S NEEDS

The purpose of expository prose is to translate the writer's thoughts into written words so that any reader will be led by the words to recreate precisely those original thoughts. If the meanings of words would only stay in place, we might be able to have some confidence in what sense readers would make of our prose; but words comprise multiple meanings which in turn increase geometrically in number when affected by different contexts, by interaction with other slippery words. This becomes further complicated when the needs of the Law are taken into consideration.

Aside from the redefinition of certain vocabulary for technical use, lawyers have no needs for language that are unique to their profession. Every need they have occurs in many other professions and situations as well. They do, however, have a special *combination* of writing needs that differs from the combination that confronts the scientist, the art historian, or any other professional.

(1) THE NEED FOR PRECISION AND ANTI-PRECISION

Lawyers constantly must seek for words that fit a given context with the greatest precision possible, even approaching a total lack of ambiguity; or, from another perspective, they must use words to shape the situation before them to best advantage. Ideally, for instance, there should never be a law suit over a contract; but at the least it is desirable that both parties know they are arguing about the same thing. At the same time, however, there is often a need to be imprecise; situations may arise in the future which cannot be conceived of at the time of drafting, and the law or agreement must be flexible enough to cover those unforeseen possibilities. This careful use of imprecision, or perhaps more accurately anti-precision, cannot be nurtured without a masterful control of precision itself. The Constitution of this country stands as a monument to the skillful use of anti-precision.

(2) THE NEED TO ARTICULATE THE STEPS AND CONNECTIONS IN A LOGICAL ARGUMENT

Poets can meaningfully juxtapose two seemingly dissimilar thoughts and challenge the reader to put them together.

> The apparition of these faces in the crowd;
> Petals, on a wet, black bough.[1]

Ezra Pound

Lawyers who do this simply invite disaster. The nature of the advocacy system demands that lawyers spell out in detail how they got from step to step in their progress towards the final conclusion. In our judge-centered court system, lawyers must make the best possible case for their side, leaving it to the judge to decide which argument is the more sound. If lawyers leave such a gap of logic between the period that ends one sentence and

---

1. Ezra Pound, "In a Station of the Metro," *Personae* (New York: New Directors, 1926), p. 109.

the capital letter that begins the next, they are doing their clients a gross disservice: in the case of a brief for a court, they are hoping the judge will come up with the connection unaided; in the case of a contract, they are hoping the other side will agree to "read in" the thoughts that never were articulated.

All too often law students fall into the trap that waits for all amateur debaters: they become so convinced of their argument that they forget to make it. To their partisan minds, a mere recitation of the facts should convince any clear thinker of the "proper" solution. ("Isn't it 'clear' that capital punishment should be abolished?") It is crucial to learn that if the process is not articulated, the product is most often meaningless.

(3) THE NEED TO RECOGNIZE THAT PEOPLE WITH VARYING VIEWPOINTS AND INTERESTS MIGHT DIFFER IN THEIR RESPONSES TO WORDS OR ARGUMENTS

Words rarely achieve objectivity by themselves. The writer must combine them or explain them to clarify the underlying intent. The man who claims he is "compassionate" might be referring to his tenderness for widows and orphans; on the other hand, he might be referring to his plan to eliminate all members of society whose I.Q. is below 90. It is not enough for the lawyer to know what he or she meant by a word or phrase; if it fails to be communicated to his audience, he or she has failed as a lawyer.

(4) THE NEED TO MAINTAIN CLARITY OF EXPRESSION, EVEN IN THE FACE OF COMPLEXITY OF THOUGHT

In order to do their business, lawyers need special words (like "demurrer" and "subrogation") and need to agree on special meanings for more common words (like "cause" and "intent"). This esoteric kind of communication, which normally baffles the layman, sometimes leads lawyers to retreat into total professional exclusivity in language. Part of a lawyer's service to the client must be the communication of what has been done, where the situation stands at present, and what can be expected of the future. This requires "plain English," not "Legalese." Even where absolute clarity is impossible, it should remain the objective.

C. AMBIGUITY AND THE LAWYER'S LANGUAGE

We encounter literally thousands of words each day, and in most cases the context will adequately define the meaning of each individual word. We therefore do not ordinarily spend a great deal of time pondering the possible ambiguities of a given word, unless the totality of the communication seems ambiguous to us. Normally we make the decision to look harder at a word or a sentence only if we are in doubt as to how to respond or proceed. The more confident we are of how to function, the less energy we expend on close reading.

Every word in our language has a wide variety of meanings —denotations, connotations, variations, vibrations, reverberations —many different ways through which it can convey meaning. When we see the word "STOP" on an octagonal red sign at the corner of the street, we understand that we are supposed to come to a halt at that point; but we also know that we do not have to remain there indefinitely, that we may go on our way as soon as we have ascertained that it is safe to do so. We also know that "STOP" applies to us only if we are driving some kind of vehicle, and that we will not receive a ticket from the police if they spot us walking past a STOP sign.

When we see the same word in the middle of a telegram, however, we hardly think of applying a brake or looking for traffic. Its meaning, although totally different from the former situation, is just as "clear" here: It replaces the final punctuation mark, the period (called the "full stop" by the British). There may be cause for confusion, however, if "STOP" appears in a telegram in a context where it could either function as a word or as a punctuational instruction. You write to your friend, "I hope you can't resist an invitation to stay with us for a day on your drive through here next week." You receive a telegram in reply: "I CANT STOP"; will you see your friend?

Only occasionally do we run into such "clever" ambiguities in daily life (despite the evidence of many a Fred Astaire movie, in which he suffers for over an hour because he has misinterpeted a message from the heroine). The lawyer, however, must deal with the possibility of ambiguity constantly, since that hostile audience will constantly be seeking for it, even when the original intention is "obvious." To add to that, the nature of Law itself makes ambiguity a difficult and everpresent problem.

Imagine the Law as the midpoint on a spectrum of ambiguity that runs from lower mathematics at one end to poetry at the other. In arithmetic there is one right answer or set of answers to every problem. The mathematical thought "means" a particular thing, and any other thing or answer is, by definition, "wrong." In poetry, at the other extreme, seeking a single right answer or meaning will lead the reader further away from rather than closer to understanding. The poet John Keats talked about this in terms of something he called "negative capability," which can be defined as the capability when faced with alternative interpretations (even mutually exclusive interpretations) not to feel compelled to choose one over the others. Not only is it not necessary to decide why Hamlet procrastinates, it is not helpful. Literature is not like a crossword puzzle which can be figured out once and then discarded. Ambiguity in poetry, therefore, must be considered a positive concept and should not be confused with "obscurity."

In terms of ambiguity, Law seems to rest directly between the two extremes of arithmetic and poetry. Like poetry, the Law constantly deals with human situations in which there is often no discernable right answer; but like arithmetic the Law is forced to produce definitive answers, which will be used in the future as the basis to solve yet other problems. The Law must do its best to find the proper compromise, which we call "justice." It must make quasi-mathematical decisions without the aid of mathematical certainty. To make things even worse, the Law is forced to use words, those quintessentially ambiguous things, to communicate its answers.

Difficult and far-reaching semantical problems can arise unexpectedly from even the simplest and best of intentions, even when there is no villainous, hostile reader to nurture them. Consider, as an example, the following statement in a will made by the hypothetical Mrs. Simple, a loving grandmother:

> I leave my entire estate in equal portions to my grandchildren.

Even without considering the problem of what may or may not be included in the estate, or how value can be assigned to all the items so that "equality" can be determined, we could spend a good deal of time trying to pin down what is meant by "grandchildren." Let us give her three children, Archibald (who married Cynthia), Tom (who married Sally), and Eugenia (who married Horace). Each couple has two children they call their own when Mrs. Simple makes her will. For each of the following situations, how many grandchildren should divide the estate? In other words, in each case who qualifies for the title "grandchild"?

(1) The two children who live with Archibald and Cynthia are Cynthia's by a previous marriage, and Archibald, who had always planned to adopt them, had not done so by the time of Mrs. Simple's death. Do they count as "grandchildren" for the purposes of the will?

(2) Six months after the death of Mrs. Simple, Archibald adopts the children. Does this change their status under the will? Would it matter if Archibald had started the adoption process before the death of his mother?

(3) Eugenia has a third child before Mrs. Simple dies. Does he share in the estate?

(4) Eugenia is pregnant with a fourth child at the time of Mrs. Simple's death. Will the new-born share in the estate?

(5) After Mrs. Simple's death, Eugenia's first child is killed. Will the estate money be redistributed?

(6) Horace becomes severely disappointed in his oldest living child, and he disowns her, saying, "You're no child of mine." Does that affect the daughter's share in the estate? Would it have made any difference if Horace had disowned her before Mrs. Simple's death?

(7) Just before Mrs. Simple's death, Tom and Sally, who had been having problems for years, decide to divorce, and Sally gets custody of the two children. Are they still Mrs. Simple's "grandchildren"?

(8) It is discovered that one of Sally's children was actually fathered by Norman, their neighbor. Tom never knew about this and therefore never legally adopted the child. Is the child still to be considered Mrs. Simple's "grandchild"?

(9) A year later Sally remarries, and her new husband, Jerome, adopts the two children. Does either child still qualify as a "grandchild"? If they do not, do they have to give up future benefits from funds invested from Mrs. Simple's estate?

(10) Tom also remarries, and with his new wife, Niobe, has seven daughters. Can the seven sisters share in the dividends which continue to accrue from the $500,000 of mutual funds that was purchased persuant to instructions in the will?

(11) A young lady named Iphegenia appears with proof that Archibald had become her foster father three years before he married Cynthia. Mrs. Simple had no knowledge of the existence of Iphy. Is she another "grandchild"?

(12) Four years after Mrs. Simple's death, a young lady named Juanita arrives, able to prove that Tom is her legal father, he having married her mother while he was in the Army years ago. The mother died before Tom returned to the States, leaving the daughter behind. Mrs. Simple had never heard about this "grandchild." Can Juanita collect?

Admittedly this family appears to need a lawyer on retainer who makes house calls every Wednesday, but any of these situations is a logical possibility, and many are commonplace happenstances nowadays. Mrs. Simple thought she knew exactly what she was doing with her estate, but what is a judge to do when Mrs. Simple is gone, and only her words remain behind?

It constantly plagues lawyers that each word in the English language denotes and connotes a myriad of meanings. When an agreement between two parties has been reduced to writing, both parties assume that they have agreed upon the specific meaning intended by each word. When a problem arises, it often concerns a disagreement in the interpretation of a word, phrase, or clause that before had seemed clear enough. If a third party, often a court, is asked to settle the matter, that party must rely upon some kind of objective standards for interpretation in order to come to a meaningful decision. The most objective of these is legal precedent, the history of how these words have been interpreted in previous cases. The Law, through its years of decision-making, has created a kind of complicated word reference system for legal use, allowing words that may have multiple or ambiguous meanings for the layman to take on specific, technical meanings for lawyers.

An example: Psychologists, philosophers, and historians have written volumes on the concept of "intent." At medical conventions psychiatrists still debate the "intentions" of famous patients of a century ago without coming to conclusive decisions. The Law, however, must always come to a decision, and it is this requirement that spawns the redefinition of words for legal purposes. Consider the following hypothetical case.

> Mr. N. Realystic learns that his girlfriend is to have a rendezvous with his worst enemy, I. B. T. Ortyme, in an abandoned shack at midnight. N. Realystic prepares a massive explosive, goes to the shack, waits until the couple is inside, and throws the explosive through the window while shouting, "I love her! I love her! I pray to God that she may be spared, for I mean her no harm. May his rotten carcass be blown to pieces." Both are killed. He is tried for first-degree murder on two counts. Did he "intend" her death?

Did not the defendant in this case clearly announce his "intention" concerning her? Or was he lying, just in case witnesses were near? Or was he perhaps not in touch with his own subconscious hostility towards her? Courts have agreed that it is not within their expertise to examine the psyche of individuals, and that for legal purposes the objective "truth" of the situation might as well not exist, if it cannot be proven. Instead they use a definition of "intention" based upon the concept of "reasonable expectations." If one can reasonably expect a certain result from one's actions, and that result does indeed happen, one is *assumed* to have "intended" the result. Whether or not this definition handles ideally all situations, it is something which the courts can use consistently and to which all sane persons can be subjected without a sense of outrage. Mr. N. Realystic therefore "intended," in the legal sense, to kill his girlfriend, just as surely as he "intended" to kill his enemy. Whenever lawyers use the word "intent" in this situation, they know what each other means, although the layman might be completely confused.

It has taken a few hundred words to communicate one part of the legal concept of "intent"; it takes only one word, "intent," to recall it for the lawyer. Tied down by these synthetic etymological bonds, lawyers cannot be expected to spell out every legal concept in the plainest of English at all times. This, however, does not excuse the profession for having developed and approved of the mystical gobbledygook we can call "Legalese" that keeps the public from understanding what is going on.

Legalese excels in two endeavors only: It obfuscates thought, and it overwhelms the non-lawyer. We can and should draw a distinction between the justified use of a specialized vocabulary and the arbitrary convoluting of syntax, diction, and meaning. When lawyers lapse into Legalese (with all of its "whereas," "witnesseth," and "heretofore" signposts), it is usually for one of four reasons:

(1) They fear that if they use "plain English" they will seem unprofessional, perhaps even incompetent;

(2) They believe that the public demands the fancy language as part of the price it pays;

(3) They feel that keeping their profession a mystery will protect and increase the public's dependence on lawyers; or

(4) They have never learned how to express themselves clearly and succinctly.

Legislatures have begun to combat Legalese by requiring that certain kinds of documents, especially those that must be understood by the population at large (pension plans, time purchase agreements, rental contracts), must be written in what they call "plain English." This has struck fear into the hearts of lawyers across the country, but not only because it will do away with the advantages of Legalese mentioned above. "Plain English" is not easy to define, not easy to write, and sometimes will not even suffice.

To complicate things further, a case will undoubtedly arise when a standard contract used in all fifty states by a commercial firm will be found to be written in perfectly "plain" English by one state's courts and yet be rejected by another's.

No matter, though, that occasional inequities and impossibilities will arise: The concept of clarifying and simplifying legal language is a sound one, and all those involved in Law, especially those beginning the study of it, should strive for control over language and greater clarity in communication of all sorts.

EXERCISE

A town ordinance reads:
No vehicles are allowed in the park. Fine: $100.

Make clear arguments concerning the following situations.

(1) Nick, a paraplegic confined to a wheel chair, wheels himself through the park. Is he breaking the law?

(2) Andrea rides her bicycle up to the park gate, reads the sign disallowing vehicles, dismounts, and walks her bike through the park. Is she breaking the law?

(3) A hurricane hits the town, knocking down several small trees and large branches in the park. The town sends members from its Park District into the park with trucks to clean up the debris and cart it away. The park will be almost unusable until this is done. Does the ordinance against vehicles in the park prohibit the clean-up project trucks?

D. TWO NOTES ON THE HISTORY OF OUR LANGUAGE

It would benefit you greatly in your understanding of words and their uses to study the history and structure of the English language. There is no space here for a detailed consideration of the subject, but the following two notes may be especially helpful to you as you review your own writing and contemplate the rhetoric of Law.

1. THE EFFECT OF THE NORMAN CONQUEST

In 1066 A.D. the Normans, who lived in what we now call France and spoke an old form of French (a Romance language), conquered the Teutonic tribes that inhabited England, who spoke Anglo-Saxon (a Teutonic language). The Normans settled in England and became the ruling class, subjugating the Saxons. Neither group was willing to adopt the language of the other, each clinging to a national identity and a class distinction, and yet they had to learn enough of each other's language to be able to communicate. Eventually the two languages molded together to form an early version of our language, with the side result of producing an unusually large number of synonyms.

The Anglo-Saxon (Teutonic) words which survived tended to be the ones that described the basic functions of life, words that a ruling class would be willing to learn so that it could make its orders known to a slave class: go, do, walk, talk, sleep, eat, live, die. They tend to be short, often only one syllable, and to simplify complex concepts. Our French (Romance) derivatives deal with the same subjects but are often longer, more complex, and make more subtle distinctions: proceed, function, perambulate, repose, ingest, survive, expire. Comparing the above two lists word for word will demonstrate the distinctions.

We have retained some of the class distinctions between the two earlier languages even to this day. Constant use of the multi-syllabic Romance vocabulary brands one either as upper class intelligencia or as simply pretentious. Inability to summon anything but Teutonic words brands one as uneducated. As a result, young students have been encouraged to write essays in "Plain English" and then make them sound sophisticated by searching through the Thesaurus for one impressively multisyllabic word per sentence, a process that produces some remarkable Malapropisms and some terribly stolid prose. Professionals who tend to fear sounding too simple gravitate towards the Romance vocabulary and, most frequently today, towards professional jargon. A return to a greater percentage of Teutonic words will not debase writing; it will allow us to get to the point more quickly and clearly and to clear up some shockingly fuzzy thinking. We should revere our Anglo-Saxon linguistic ancestors as much as our Norman ones; to deny the former is to try to make the language something it has never been. Seek out the blunt and straightforward word, unless the situation calls for a distinction that is handled more deftly and aptly by a Romance word. Above all, rid yourself of the false concept that a cosmetic displacing of vocabulary (a substituting of a fancy word for a plain one) has anything to do with revision and the improving of prose, which can only be accomplished by the improving of thought first.

2. THE TRANSLATION OF THE LAW INTO ENGLISH

Legal language in England underwent two major translations, from Latin to Law French (13th Century) and from Law French to English (early 16th Century), the latter of which has left a curious mark on our present legal terminology. Law French, a curious mixture of Latin, English, and French, was the language of international trade in northwest Europe during the early Middle Ages. The merchants of the 13th Century had studied little Latin (in which the laws of that time were written) and were reluctant to entrust all their affairs to those few who knew the older language. Therefore they managed to have all the important legal documents translated into the language they did know, and within a few decades the process was complete, Latin being relegated to Church Law only.

In the two centuries that followed, a great many questions of law were decided for the first time. Terms were defined and principles established, all of which necessitated the forging of a specialized legal vocabulary. By the 16th Century Law French had become a highly technical language in its legal uses, but had faded away substantially as a language for international trade. Once again the merchants found themselves somewhat out of touch with the language that defined the regulations under which they must function, and once again they pressed to have the laws translated, this time into English. Henry VIII was willing to make the change, but he was faced with a problem that had not beset the earlier translation from Latin: Legal vocabulary had become so specialized that words well known to the lay population would mean completely different things to a lawyer. It was feared that by translating the Law French into English, the specialized distinctions which had taken so long to build up, would be lost, or, at the least, that great confusion would follow. Would the new English word mean everything that the word meant to a layman, or would it bring with it only the meanings known to the lawyers?

To avoid confusion, therefore, some Law French terms were both retained and translated, thereby making two synonymous words do the work originally done by one. For example, the Law French "testament" was translated into the English "will"; but because "will" might suggest a good deal more than "testament" had included, the two words were grafted together. We still use this redundant phrase: "last will and testament", which refers to one document, not two. A large number of these duplications has survived, some of which follow. Note how many combine a monosyllabic Teutonic word with multisyllabic Romance words.

null and void
cease and desist
full and complete
good and sufficient
made and entered into
save and except
give, devise and bequeath
rest, residue and remainder

Chapter II

A SYSTEM FOR SELF-REVISION: THE TYRANNY OF THE WEAK VERB

A. THE WEAK VERB

The purpose of an expository composition is to expose the thoughts of a writer. Ideally the process includes both a conversion and a reconversion: A writer converts thoughts into words so that a reader can reconvert those words into precisely the original thoughts. This differs from the purpose of a poem, novel, or play, all of which may elicit responses as numerous as their readers. If expository compositions (directions to the San Diego Zoo or a brief for the Supreme Court) allow for multiple interpretations, they have failed in their primary purpose.

Once the writer has completed a rough draft, his major problem becomes discerning which of his sentences will communicate accurately and which will not. As he struggles to be his own editor, however, his mind deceives him and robs him of objectivity. The following seems to happen: He looks at the words; he recalls their individual denotations and connotations; he understands the significance of the syntax; and synthesizing all of this he perceives a meaning for the whole sentence. If that meaning corresponds to his intended meaning (and it usually does), he proceeds to the next sentence. Actually, however, the following happens: He recognizes the words and the order they are in; he remembers what he was thinking when he put those words in that order. Since this has brought to mind for him his intended meaning, he believes it will do the same for his reader and therefore proceeds to the next sentence. Mere association, and not objective perception, has produced the desired self-satisfaction. Had the writer spilled coffee on his manuscript in the fervor of recording some brilliant insight at the breakfast table, that coffee stain might perform the same associative function for him; for years to come

18

it might bring that insight immediately to his mind. It is highly unlikely to do that for his reader.

This paints a rather bleak picture. If one can never escape the dangers of mere association, then how can one ever judge objectively and therefore improve one's own writing? Fortunately, however, there do exist reliable "danger signals" in writing which consistently indicate that something is malfunctioning in a sentence. If the writer eradicates the offending "signals," the chances of the sentence communicating accurately increase dramatically.

Thought and expression of thought (in this case, writing) are so inextricably intertwined that the quality of either one reflects the quality of the other. Therefore good writing (by which I mean writing that effectively communicates, not writing that merely impresses) cannot exist in the absence of good thought. Conversely, poor writing indicates a lack of clarity or care in thought. Although it might not help to be told to go home and "think better," it will help to be given a system by which you can remove these objectively perceivable dangers, which will, in turn, help to clarify your thought process.

This system of self-revision is sophisticated and difficult to use, but much worth the effort. You need apply it in detail only a few times to benefit from it; by then you will understand its principles well enough to encorporate them in your initial writing process. It deals with no mere cosmetic concerns; instead it gives you a way of penetrating to the core of the thought that set you writing in the first place. It is only reasonable, therefore, that such a process of reconstruction would require a substantially strenuous effort.

The most serious and most frequently encountered "danger signal" is the weak main verb. For the purposes of this system, I define "weak verb" as a verb whose meaning has little or no relationship to the meaning of the sentence as a whole. Conversely, a strong verb is one whose meaning bears a direct relationship to the meaning of the sentence as a whole. It follows that no verb is strong or weak by itself, but only in the way it is used. Since every verb has a meaning, and that meaning might conceivably dominate the thought of a particular sentence, then every verb is potentially strong. Example: Consider the following sentence, written as the climax of an 800-page novel:

"Jack actually articulated his love for Jill."

Is "articulated" a weak or a strong verb? We cannot tell until we know what the sentence is trying to say. If throughout the novel Jack's problem has always been his inability to feel strong emotion for someone else, then "articulated" would be a weak verb. His ability to love Jill outweighs in importance his ability to articulate it. If throughout the novel, on the other hand, Jack has been a passionate sort but has never been able to express his feelings openly, then "articulated" would be a far stronger choice than "love" for the main verb.

In English, the main verb controls the structure and therefore the meaning of the sentence. All words in the main clause depend on it directly; all subordinate clauses relate to it directly or indirectly. The soundness of the sentence as a whole therefore depends directly on the strength of the main verb.

This does not hold true for all languages because linguistic structures differ so.   In Latin, for example, the main verb appears most often at the end of the sentence. Had the main verb been the structural control for Latin, the Romans would have been in the dark about every sentence uttered until just after it was over. Instead they used "inflections," word endings which indicated the relationships between that word and the others in the sentence. If they wished to say "Jack loves Jill," they would put an ending on "Jack" ("u," indicating masculinity, and "s," designating him as the doer of the action), an ending on "Jill" ("a," indicating femininity, and "m," designating her as the object of the action), and an ending on the verb *amo*, "to love" ("-at," showing the action is done in the present by a third person singular agent). Result:

Jackus Jillam amat ("Jack loves Jill").

Any ordering of these Latin words, such as

Jillam amat Jackus

or

amat Jackus Jillam

would still produce the concept of "Jack loves Jill" because the "-s" and the "-m" endings proclaim those words to be, respectively, subject and object. Despite the word order, he will always remain the lover and she the lovee. In English, as many a novel has made clear, "Jack loves Jill" can differ dramatically from "Jill loves Jack."

In English we depend on word order for our syntactical structure, and the placement and choice of the main verb dictate the arrangement of the rest of the sentence. Yet most people do not choose their verb first and then proceed to construct the sentence around it, as the needs of the English language would seem to dictate. Instead they compose a sentence in linear fashion, beginning with the first word (most often the sentence's subject) and proceeding from there. The choice of subject usually determines the choice of predicate, and the writer ends by stuffing a verb in between as a mere grammatical necessity. (As a result, one of the most common writing errors is the "sentence fragment," a string of words that lacks a verb.)

The system I suggest is based upon the notion that the stronger the verb is, the healthier the sentence will tend to be. Choose the verb whose meaning is most directly connected to the meaning of the thought as a whole, and the rest of the sentence will fall naturally into place.

Let us look more closely at the difference between weak and strong verbs, taking special note of the nature of the passive construction, after which will follow the procedure for utilizing these concepts in revising one's own writing.

Again, no verb is weak or strong by itself, but only by its usage; but of all verbs, people use "to be" ("am," "are," "is," etc.) weakly more often than any other. "To be" has two major meanings, "exists" and "equals," and when a writer intends either of those as his main thought, he is using the verb strongly. "God is": the verb's meaning goes straight to the heart of the matter (the existence of God), making it a strong verb. "Property is theft," said George Bernard Shaw: another strong usage, for who would have guessed before reading the sentence that the two nouns "equalled" each other? But most of the time when "is" means "equals," that is when it means "the words before me and the words after me have something in common," the writer has only gathered materials for a sentence and has not clearly understood what he or she wants to communicate. You would probably be quite surprised at the number of "to be"'s you use. Investigate: for one of your recent essays underline all the main verbs, being careful to treat all passive constructions as "to be" (treating the participle as only a verbal adjective). Then compute the percentage of "to be"'s. The resulting statistic will show you why we can use "is" as a prototypical example of the weakly used verb.

What is wrong with weak verbs? Consider the following analogy from algebra. If I gave you this series of equations:

$$\text{Series I:} \quad 2a^2 + 3b^2 = 30$$
$$a^2 - b^2 = 5$$

you could, after brushing up on some early algebra, "develop" the mathematical thought by putting "a^2" in terms of "b^2" in one equation, transferring that value to the other equation, and performing the mathematical functions indicated. You would discover "answers," namely that "a" equals plus or minus 3, and "b" equals plus or minus 2.

If, on the other hand, I asked you to develop the mathematical thought in this second series of equations:

$$\text{Series II:} \quad a = b$$
$$b = c$$
$$c = d$$
$$d = e$$

you could reply only that all the unknowns were equal. You might wonder why I had bothered to distinguish "a" from "b" or "c" or "d" or "e" in the first place.

If I went one step further and asked you to respond to this third series of equations:

$$\text{Series III:} \quad a = b$$
$$c = d$$
$$e = f$$

you would be justified in complaining that you could learn nothing at all from it. Such a gap of logic exists between the equations that no mathematical meaning surfaces.

When you write a series of sentences constantly utilizing weak verbs, your writing resembles either Series II or Series III above. In the former case you force yourself to repeat something major from the immediately preceding sentence before you can develop a new sentence. Having defined or labeled "b" as being "a," you must restate "b" before continuing your thought. An exaggerated example:

a = b	The sky is blue.
b = c	Blue is a color.
c = d	Color is produced by light. . . .

A more common example:

a = b	I am in college now because an education will be good for me.
b = c	An education is an opportunity to learn many things.
c = d	Learning many things will allow me to choose better what I want to do in life.

A seemingly more sophisticated example:

a = b	The party of the first part will be in contact with the party of the second part once each month.
b = c	On the 15th of the month the party of the second part will receive from the party of the first part full monthly payment according to the contract.
c = d	The monthly payment will be applied to the base cost of operation and the residue will be applied to the reserve account.

In all these examples thought seems to be going somewhere, but actually it is merely running in place. Each sentence tacks itself onto the one before, and precious little substance emerges from the morass of words.

The situation worsens when the paragraph takes on a Series III construction. An exaggerated example:

a = b	The sky was clear.
c = d	I was able to go to the beach.
e = f	Mark got to drive the convertible.

Many a reader could piece together a story from this, but would it necessarily be the same as the one in the writer's mind? A more common example, from an actual Freshman paper:

> a = b   It was clear that I should go to college.
>
> c = d   State U. seemed to be the best choice.
>
> e = f   I got to live in the dorm, and there is a neat intramural athletic program.

When this sorry method tackles sophisticated material, the resulting maze of words can take the heart out of the most enthusiastic reader. Pity the client of the investment analyst who had to deal with this:

> Committed facilities can be made available for periods up to, say, seven years. The assurance that such a facility remains available for drawings for a specified period is achieved by the payment of a commitment fee which, typically, is payable only on the unused portion of the line. This represents an attractive alternative to a domestic line at a prime rate plus compensating balances because the cost of a commitment fee is normally equivalent to, say, 10% of the line; and, of course, to the extent that the line is used no commitment fee at all is payable.

Even if you understood the technical language used, you would have a difficult time understanding what he was trying to convey.

Although the last example seems more complex than the earlier ones, the causes of its low quality do not differ from theirs. When you write Series III type sentences, you fail to fulfill your primary function as an expository writer, which, once again, is to convert thoughts into words in such a way that the reader of those words will be led to recreate precisely your original thoughts. Instead you are saying, "Reader, here is a sentence, and here is another, and here is a third. You figure out why I put them together in this order." The unbridgable gap between the period that ends one sentence and the capital letter that begins the next confounds the reader. To write in that manner is to abrogate your solemn duty to tell the reader as clearly as possible what to do with the words on the page, how to put them together, what they might mean in this given instance, and how they relate to previous uses of them on the same page.

Poets can communicate most effectively without these restrictions, by juxtaposing words and letting them reverberate differently for each reader. However, the poem, once written, no longer belongs to the poet; it is the unique property of each individual who reads it, siphoning it through his or her personal experience. Expository prose demands just the opposite. Ideally, every reader should grasp exactly the same meaning that the writer had in mind. The writer's ideas, and not the reader's interpretations, should dominate.

Let us consider the structure of a weak verb sentence in the abstract. We construct the simplest one possible by placing a weak "to be" between a subject and predicate (such as "Roses are flowers" or "Roses are red"). We can represent this by:

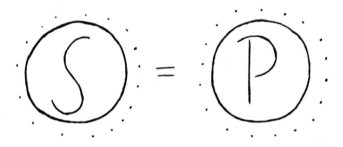

The dots surrounding "S" and "P" represent the myriad of possible meanings each word might have if considered in isolation: denotations, connotations, vibrations, variations, reverberations, any -ations you like. No reader could guess precisely which aspect of "Roses" I might have in mind, if only "Roses" appeared on the paper. The same would hold true for "flowers," were that the only word printed. When I join these two words only by an "is," I do no more than invite the reader to make a judicious guess at what I perceive to be "equal" about the two words.

The result can be a minor disaster in communication. My meaning might appear to me most clear:

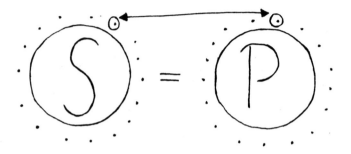

whereas my reader might just as reasonably construe the sentence:

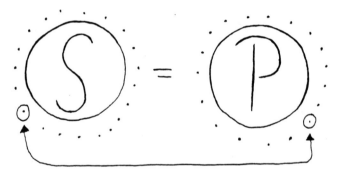

I have shirked my responsibility. I have not directed my reader
clearly enough how to relate the subject to the predicate. I have
given no instructions and asked the reader to perform no specific
functions. "Here is 'Roses,' dear Reader, and here is 'flowers.'
I leave it to you to figure out what is 'equal' about them.
I do hope we agree."

Now consider the sentence whose verb is strong, whose verb capsulizes the main meaning of the sentence as a whole: "Jack loves Jill." We can represent this as:

Once again each word has multiple possible meanings, but in this case each word is limited by those with which it interacts. What aspect of Jack, what kind of Jack are we talking about here?—the kind that is capable of loving; what quality of Jill? —the sort of Jill that can be loved; what kind of "love"?—the kind of emotion that this Jack is capable of feeling for this Jill. The meanings of the words interact like cogs in a machine and produce a composite meaning that is more immediately identifiable by the reader.

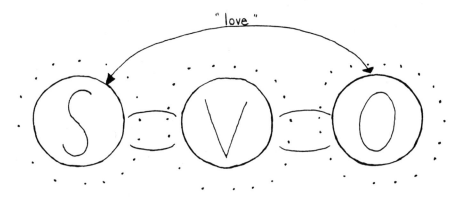

What is the relationship between Jack and Jill here? It is one of "love." What is the relationship between "Roses" and "flowers" above? You guess, Reader, and if you are lucky, you will have hit upon my meaning.

By using a strong verb you tell your readers how to construct connections between the other elements of the sentence. By using a weak verb you force your readers to do too much guess-work, and you depend on the questionable probability that their response to those words resembles yours. This can be especially disastrous in the field of Law, where most of your readers will be either adversaries or devil's advocates, intentionally seeking to misread you.

The use of weak verbs breeds weak thought processes and diminishes the chances for accurate communication. Choosing strong verbs not only improves those chances, but it forces the writer to consider more carefully the nature and progression of the thought process, thereby strengthening both.

B. A NOTE ON THE PASSIVE

Writing teachers and texts usually warn against excessive use of the passive on the grounds that it is "weak" or "not as direct," which suggests there are stylistically stronger ways of making the same point in the active. I would submit that the passive does far more serious damage to writing: It tends to smooth out rhythms and elongate sentences to make them sound full of grace when they are actually void of sense.

The passive reverses the roles of subject and object. In the active, the subject is the doer of the action, and the object is that person or thing to whom the action is done.

Jack hit Jill.

In the passive, the object of the action takes the grammatical position of the subject and vice versa, necessitating the transformation of the active verb ("hit") into the passive verb, formed by "to be" plus a participle ("is hit").

Jill is hit by Jack.

If we consider the participle as merely a verbal adjective, then all passive constructions, with a few exceptions that I will note below, must be "weak" by my definition, for the main thrust of the sentence will usually reside in the concept of the action ("hit") and not in the subject's state of "being." Sentences using the passive, therefore, will usually suffer all the dangers of any other sentences that feature weak main verbs.

We tend to use the form a great deal only because the active version of the same thought betrays how little content we have covered in the sentence. An example may help to clarify this. Responding to an assignment to define the term "football team," one student began his paper with the following lacklustre but seemingly reasonable statement:

Football is a game played by two football teams.

As underwhelming as this sentence is, it still does seem to open the topic for consideration and get the paper on track. If we look closely at it, we probably will criticize the writer for trying to define "football" in terms of "football," not a helpful process for his reader.

If we cure the sentence of its passivity by transforming it into the active, its true depth of emptiness glistens before our eyes. To make a passive sentence active, exchange the functions of the subject and the object, delete the verb "to be," and make the participle into the main verb. In this case we find:

Two football teams play the game football.

The rhythms no longer lull us into non-recognition. The sentence ends with a klunk after a short stumble. We see once more that he has defined "football" in terms of "football," but we also see the redundancy of "play" and "game." He leaves the word "team," one of his main definitional targets, totally unexplained. He might as well have told us that "Two football glops play the game football." He gives us only one concrete bit of information in the whole sentence: "two." Whatever "teams" may be, it takes two of them to "play the game football."

Two football teams play the game football.

This transformation process neither introduced new material into the rewrite of this sentence nor excluded old material; it merely uncovered the previously camouflaged emptiness of meaning.

Read the two sentences again, aloud:

Football is a game played by two football teams.

Two football teams play the game football.

You can hear a difference, and yet there is no substantial difference. Whenever you find yourself tempted to use the passive, rewrite the sentence in the active so that you may better judge its depth and breadth, or lack of same.

There are a few strong uses of the passive, however, and when carefully used the construction can be most effective.

(1) When you are ignorant of the identity of the agent of the action:

Passive:

The bomb was left in the marketplace sometime between Noon and one o'clock.

Active:

Someone left the bomb in the marketplace sometime between Noon and one o'clock.

(2) When you wish to emphasize the result instead of the cause:

Passive:

My plate glass window was broken this afternoon, neighbor.

Active:

Someone broke my window this afternoon, neighbor.

The passive here sounds less accusative. It gives the neighbor the opportunity to suggest, gracefully, that his child was at fault.

(3) When you wish to emphasize the fact that a causative reason is unknown:

Passive:

I am moved to tears by Beethoven's music, but I do not know why.

Active:

I do not know why Beethoven's music moves me to tears.

The use of the passive underscores this mystery.

(4) When you wish to indicate that the subject ought to be in control of the action and is at fault for not being so:

> *Passive:*
>
> The professor is led by his theory to the following ridiculous conclusion.
>
> *Active:*
>
> The professor's theory leads him to the following ridiculous conclusion.

Both sentences work well enough, but the former shames the professor more than the second because of his unwitting passivity. He ought to be in control of where his theories go, but he has somehow lost his dominance, as the passive structure emphasizes.

(5) When you and/or your reader are the perpetrator(s) of the action, but you wish your reader to forget this and concentrate on the rest of the information:

> *Passive:*
>
> In this course the nature of Symbolism will be considered. Works by X, Y, and Z will be read.
>
> *Active:*
>
> I will consider the nature of Symbolism in this course. You will read works by X, Y, and Z.

In the active form, the "I" sounds too manipulative and the "You" sounds too oppressed. The passive sentence puts the emphasis on the educational process instead of the sovereign-serf relationship.

In almost all other cases than those noted here, the active will serve you better. If the active sounds embarrassingly klunky to you, rejoice in your discovery of a rotten sentence and rehabilitate the thing. Add some thought.

C. THE SYSTEM

This system offers a relatively objective method by which you can overcome major problems and discover for yourself how much of your thought actually has reached the paper. It involves mainly the removing of the two worst "danger signals" in writing: (1) The weak main verb; and (2) the repetition of major words or phrases (including synonyms). It is a strenuous and trying process to undergo, but even its unpleasantness serves a positive function, as I shall explain below. Meticulous use of it on only a few papers will awaken you to your own writing process well enough that you will no longer make the errors the system sets out to correct. In other words, we have here a positive use of planned obsolescence. You should apply the system to one paragraph at a time. I set out the steps here and follow them with a detailed example which should help greatly to elucidate them.

Step 1

Circle the main verb(s) in each clause of each sentence, being careful to treat all passive constructions as the verb "to be." If you cannot deduce the general topic of the paragraph from reading only the circled words, then you have too many weak verbs and should continue to Step 2.

Step 2

Considering only the first sentence, decide if the main verb(s) communicates the central idea. If it does not, decide what the most important content of the sentence is and find a verb that capsulizes that idea. Then restructure a sentence around the new main verb, being extremely careful to include everything from your original sentence and to add nothing that is new (at this point).

Often in the restructuring of a sentence some element of the original simply will not fit the new schema. If this happens, note the word or words in the margin so you can return to them later. The marginalia often prove crucial in discovering the underlying motivations that led to the sentence in the first place. Most probably you were trying to say two different things at the same time. This rewrite will force you to choose the more important one and discard the other for the moment. Eventually you will be led to consider why you tried so hard to combine the two thoughts in the first place, at which time you can articulate that reason and expand on it. Sometimes the very heart of a paragraph's thought shows through only via the separating and recombining of the marginalia.

In trying to decide what the sentence was really trying to say, you might ask which of the words in it is the most important and then make a verb out of that. Example:

This sentence is a good example of the point I am trying to make.

"Example" strikes me as the most important word in that sentence. To rewrite, we make "example" into a verb, "exemplify," and restructure everything else around it:

This sentence exemplifies my point well.

Important warning: Do not try to replace the weak verb with one that looks more fancy, leaving the rest of the sentence as it was. If the verb is weak, the strength of the sentence lies elsewhere and will continue to do so, no matter what word is dropped into the slot vacated by the departing weak verb. In this revision we are altering the structure of the sentence, not merely upgrading the diction; we are after a total reconstruction job, not just cosmetic surgery.

Another important warning: Be precise concerning the admonitions to include everything from the original sentence and to add nothing new. If you leave out something you had written before, you are disregarding what could be a central clue to your previous thought process. If you add anything that was not there before, you are developing your thoughts in a different order than you had previously and may run into difficulties in the following sentences and paragraphs. It is enough of a task to revise one sentence's thought at a time.

Step 3

Repeat Step 2 for each sentence in the paragraph, being careful to treat each one in isolation. The more completely you can disregard all other sentences while working on one, the better your final result will be.

Step 4

Now reread your new sentences as a new paragraph and take note of the large number of repetitions that have surfaced. (Your main verbs will repeat, as well as your subjects, in most cases.) Then combine sentences to eliminate as many of the repeats as you can. During this process you should attempt to add in all the words you relegated to the margins earlier. You will find yourself reordering thoughts and articulating connections you had previously omitted, thus filling in the "gap between the period that ends one sentence and the capital letter that begins the next."

Step 5

If the process of collapsing redundancies leaves your sentences with seemingly less of your thought that you felt you were trying to express before, search your prose throughout these drafts for patterns that might have been forming. For example, check all the subjects of sentences. Do they form a pattern or progression? Do the same for the verbs, the objects, and the modifiers. Have you included a large number of abstract nouns, or of any other recognizable category of words? Are they in a pattern? The sample paragraph investigated below will help clarify this point.

Step 6

Polish the prose so that it fulfills grammatical requirements and proceeds as smoothly, directly, and forcefully as possible.

This whole process demands a "leap of faith" on your part. You must assume that you would not have bothered to record on paper any sentence—or even word—that had no purpose. The system allows you the opportunity to discover more fully what it was you were trying to say in the first place. Your first draft becomes a cache of clues to this mystery, and the five steps I have outlined facilitate the unweaving of the plot.

The condemnation of repetition intends to make you aware of another insidious process. When we have written a sentence that has not fully articulated our thought, instead of repairing the original, we tend to add another sentence, backing up, as it were, for another running start at the thing. Often the second attempt also fails, and we try for a third time. All this while, we are under the impression that we are "developing" thought, whereas actually we are stuck on the ice, spinning our wheels, unwittingly disguising the same thought in two or three different semantic packages. If we have spoken three times about the same subject, most likely the relationship between the three statements concerns us the most, but it is precisely that relationship we have neglected to state explicitly. By ridding the paragraph of major repetitions, we force ourselves to articulate how the different statements overlap and relate.

To make the abstract more tangible, let us look closely at the system in action, a revision of a paragraph written in response to an assignment to describe a riot scene in about 50 words. Keep in mind, though, that for this demonstration you are only a spectator and therefore will not necessarily be able to guess what the best version of any sentence should be. Only the author knows what she meant by a given phrase, so only the author can choose the appropriate strong verb to express it. Do not be surprised, therefore, if she chooses to emphasize something that seems less than centrally important to you; she will just be demonstrating how inaccurately she had communicated her intentions the first time. Here is her paragraph:

> A riot is developed when a group of people gathers together in a public place with opposing views towards one idea. This is usually accomplished in a way that disturbance is created. Confusion, loud outbursts, and violence are most likely to happen. In some riots a person could even be killed.

It looked to me as if she had spent no more than ten minutes and had expended no emotional energy whatever on this assignment. I was puzzled when she told me how many hours and how much grief it had cost her. Even so, the writing seemed dull to me, an unpromising candidate for exciting revision; but since weak verbs dominated throughout, I knew something good would come from using the system, even if only neatness and concision. We went ahead with the process.

Step 1

Her main verbs were "is," "gathers," "is," "is," "are," and "could be." Since we could tell nothing about the paragraph as a whole from reading only these verbs, we proceeded to the next steps.

Steps 2 and 3

We reconstructed her sentences individually, searching for the most important elements in each, transforming those into main verbs, and then reconstructing the sentences, being careful to work on only one sentence at a time.

#1 Old: A riot is developed when a group of people gathers together in a public place with opposing views towards one idea.

Because of its length, we split this sentence at first into its three component parts:

(a) A riot is developed—

She felt the concept of "develop" had been her central consideration. Making it into a main verb, we produced:

(a) A riot develops—

(b) when a group of people gathers together in a public place—

Here she felt that her verb, "gathers," had indeed expressed her thought. We were going to leave the phrase unchanged, but she at the last moment asked if we could "neaten it up" by taking out "together," a seemingly redundant word, since it would be impossible for a group to "gather apart." Since the system requires that everything from the original must be conserved through this revision stage, we did not get rid of "together," but exiled it instead to the margin. She then recorded the following for segment (b):

(b) when groups of people gather in a public place—

I complained that she had again made a substantial change, transforming the singular "group" into the plural "groups." She insisted on the change, again on the basis of "neatness." We compromised, adding to our marginalia the notation "group/groups."

(c) with opposing views towards one idea.

She chose "oppose" as the main idea and produced:

(c) people oppose each other's views on one idea.

We then recombined the three fragments into one grammatical whole:

#1 New: A riot develops when groups of people gather in a public place to oppose each other's views on one idea. (Marginalia: "together," and "group/groups.")

#2 Old: This is usually accomplished in a way that disturbance is created.

She opted for "creation" as having been her main intention for communication here. Using "creates" as her verb, she reconstructed "this" as the subject, "a disturbance" as the object, and retained the adverb "usually." The words "in a way that" can be dismissed because the transformation of the sentence from passive to active takes away their function entirely. She had trouble, however, accommodating the word "accomplished," which began to seem a strange word to use in describing a riot. Can one be said to have "accomplished" a riot that one had not intended to incite? We relegated "accomplished" to the margin for the time being.

#2 New: This usually creates a disturbance. (Marginalia: "accomplished.")

#3 Old: Confusion, loud outbursts, and violence are most likely to happen.

She could find no single word in this sentence that adequately expressed what she had been aiming at. "Happen" seemed too haphazard; "most likely" came closer to the sense of "one thing having to lead to another," as she put it. She finally chose "lead" to express the thought, and using the phrase "in turn" to express the force of her original word "usually," she wrote down the following:

#3 New: This, in turn, usually leads to confusion, outbursts, and violence.

I suggested that she had neglected to copy the word "loud." She became slightly upset when I started to add it, insisting that the nice progression of three abstract words would be marred by the inclusion of an adjective for only one of them. "Loud," she felt, "broke the rhythm." I could not understand why she should be so adamant about this detail. Since she was the author, we excluded it from the sentence; but since the system disallows the discarding of original material, we included it in the marginalia.

#4 Old: In some riots a person could even be killed.

I would have been willing to give odds that "killed" would be her choice as most important word in this sentence, but I would have lost my bet. She once again decided that the concept of "lead" had been uppermost in her mind. Therefore she produced:

#4 New: Rioting can even lead to killing.

At the end of Step 3, her paragraph looked like this:

A riot develops when groups of people gather in a public place to oppose each other's views on one idea. This usually creates a disturbance. This in turn usually leads to confusion, outbursts, and violence. Rioting can even lead to killing.

The marginalia included "together," "group/groups," "accomplished," and "loud." Her main verbs now told us something about the paragraph all by themselves: "develops," "gather," "creates," "leads," and "can lead." She discovered that she actually had been trying to write about the developmental aspects of rioting, how one thing of necessity "leads" to another.

STEP 4

We tried to cut out the repetitions of the concept of "leading" or "developing." We found there were two major parts to her thought:

(1) People gather in a public place to disagree;
(2) The disagreements lead to physical violence of some proportions.

We could express this in a single sentence:

When people gather in public places to disagree on ideas, the confusion can often result in serious physical violence.

STEP 5

It seemed that through our efforts at concision we had somehow impoverished her original paragraph, for she felt strongly that her previous description had said a good deal more than did this capsulization. Therefore we looked hard at what we had discarded in the process. We found the missing material not in her individual sentences, but in the progressions she had established but not clearly articulated.

We looked for any patterns that she had developed but that had fallen victim to the "collapsing the redundancies" process. We found first that the abstract nouns she had used to describe the riot had proceeded in a logical order from mild disorder to serious disorder.

> "disturbance"
> "confusion"
> "outbursts"
> "violence"
> "killing"

This too she had structured from her central concept of "development," and it depicted a societal disintegration. Each term in the series added to the concreteness of the concept: The abstract "disturbance" gave way to the more visual and auditory "confusion," which was in turn focussed yet more in terms of the more specific (in sound and duration of sound) "outbursts." Then "violence" added the sense of touch, and "killing" made all the generalities specific, as the effects of the whole lighted upon individual persons.

And more: She saw the unities at the beginning of the paragraph turning to disunities by the end. People were "gathering together" concerning "one" idea at the beginning. By the end the general confusion was resulting in the death of individuals. She discovered she had been struggling with another major idea, paradoxical to what was going on both in the riot and in the rest of the paragraph. People, she felt, ought to gather, ought to discuss, in order to build a better societal unit. The tragedy of rioting lay in the irony: precisely that action that was to have brought people together resulted in tearing them apart. Where there should have been progress and unification, there was only disintegration and death. Suddenly the word "together," which we had relegated to the margin, made sense: She had indeed been writing a description of people "gathering apart," something we had considered impossible before. At least, when they gathered "together" it had the effect of tearing them "apart."

Two other clues from the marginalia supported her having had these conflicting feelings about the riot scene from the start. She discovered a possible motivation for her having changed "group" to "groups" in our rewrite: The singular, "group," expressed her initial hope that people could come together in unity, but the plural, "groups," described the actuality that resulted. People had come to the scene in separate groups, and the hoped for unity never materialized. When she wrote the beginning of her original paragraph, she had taken herself back to the beginning of the riot scene she had witnessed personally. By the time of the rewrite, she had relived the experience and had suffered again the loss of her original optimism. The hoped for single "group" had become transformed into the actual multiplicity of "groups."

Second, she was still troubled that she had used such a positive word as "accomplished" (and even the mostly positive "created") in the midst of a statement about disintegration. Now she saw that her feelings while writing the original paragraph truly had been mixed; she was going in both directions at the same time, towards the "accomplishments" she had hoped for and the "disturbance" that had eventuated.

And more: We looked at the subjects throughout the paragraph, all abstracts, especially the "This" of the second and third sentences. I asked her what she was referring to by the use of "this." She answered, "It—you know, the violence, the disruption." Why, I asked her, had she not named the agents who perpetrated all this violence? Why not talk about them directly? She was troubled by the question. "Well, because it was really nobody's 'fault.' I mean, no one person was 'to blame.' It just sort of started. It took over." Beyond the frustrated feeling of paradox, she had been considering also the perplexing question of guilt, and she was refusing to allocate any blame whatsoever. She accomplished that by removing all traces of agency, by making the subjects of her sentences as impersonal as possible. Also she was reflecting, she felt, her major dread concerning riots, that people start "it," but eventually "it" takes over and is no longer controllable.

I never would have believed, just from reading her original paragraph, that she had ever witnessed a riot in person. The prose on its surface seemed so remote, so uninvolved. As we continued to dig under that surface, I began to understand how she could have spent several hours of anxiety over its creation.

By this time she was totally engrossed in her memories of that riot. She suggested that the impersonality in her description had also stemmed from wanting to keep the whole experience of writing at arm's length, since the experience of watching had upset her so. Suddenly she looked awed and said, "That's why I took out the 'loud'!". It had recreated the memory too vividly for her. Without the "loud," the paper for her would refer to any old riot, not necessarily hers. She was editing out, indeed, repressing, a painful reminder.

In summary: The four seemingly innocent sentences she had started with led her to a five-page paper about the order in which things get out of hand (the central paradox). It explored the positive things that might have happened and the irony of the negative things that actually happened. It talked about the difficulties of being involved and the ways in which memory haunts you afterwards. It talked about dreams, failures, and realities. It was a wonderful paper.

This was no solitary fluke. I have seen similar unfoldings of ideas and associations literally hundreds of times while applying this system. It involves neither luck nor magic; it simply is a step-by-step way of asking yourself what you really meant to say in the first place. When you try to rid the sentence of its weak verb, you force yourself to reconsider what it was you thought was centrally important when you were constructing the original sentence. When you try to rid the paragraph of redundancies, you force yourself to review how all those ideas seemed to you to relate to each other in the first place. When you try to make sense of the materials you earlier relegated to the margins, you force yourself to unearth the relationships they could possibly have had to your topic as a whole. In short, through the revision process you gain perspective on the thought process that motivated you to write in the first place.

Nothing in this book is of greater importance than the system just described. Go back through this chapter, several times if necessary, until you are thoroughly familiar with how it works and why. Then force yourself to use it in detail for the next few papers you write. You will find you need to use it less and less as you come to understand it more and more. Eventually you can discard all the details of the system and just concentrate on strong verbs.

In time this system will improve not only the quality of your writing, but also the speed of your composing process and even the force of your oral communication. It will accomplish this, strangely enough, through its sheer unpleasantness. Replacing weak verbs with strong ones, and constantly asking yourself "What did I mean to say?", are such distasteful tasks that you will quickly learn to stop using weak verbs in your composing process so that you can avoid the future pain of having to replace them. You will even begin to form thoughts in terms of strong verbs, to think more immediately in terms of what you mean to say. I repeat: Thought and expression of thought are so inextricably intertwined that the quality of either one reflects the quality of the other.

EXERCISE

(1) Based upon your understanding of this chapter, criticize the following attempt by a first-year law student to write an argument against California's Therapeutic Abortion Act.

    (a) What in general is wrong with the language of the memo? What has the writer failed to do, and why?

    (b) What "danger signals" do you see operating in the prose?

    (c) What happens if *you* try to correct this prose with the system explained in this chapter? (Hint: try it and see.) What is the significance of this?

    (d) What has the writer succeeded in communicating?

Note: Section 274 of California's Penal Code States: "Every person who procures the miscarriage of a woman, except as provided in the Therapeutic Abortion Act . . . is punishable by imprisonment . . .."

The Therapeutic Abortion Act provides that

    (a) a licensed physician and surgeon is authorized to perform an abortion in an accredited hospital

    (b) if it is approved in advance by the hospital committee, and

    (c) if the committee finds that one or both of the following conditions exist:

        (1) substantial risk to the mother's health if pregnancy continues;

        (2) the pregnancy resulted from incest or rape.

Another section provides that an abortion may be approved on the grounds of statutory rape only if the girl is under the age of 15 years. Yet another section, #252953, states that the hospital committee must consist of not less than two licensed physicians and surgeons; but if the proposed termination of pregnancy will occur after the 13th week, the committee must consist of three such physicians and surgeons.

Here is the student's argument:

I feel that Penal Code section 274 should be repealed because parts of the Therapeutic Abortion Act are arbitrarily laid down for no reason at all.

Since the Therapeutic Abortion Act is the exception of Penal Code 274, it is an interconnected part of it. That is, wherever Penal Code section 274 does not apply, the exception, the Therapeutic Abortion Act, applies. The question, therefore, is whether the Therapeutic Abortion Act is applicable. I feel that it is not, because parts of it are arbitrarily laid down for no reason at all.

In order for Penal Code section 274 to be established, parts of the Therapeutic Abortion Act must be amended. Part (c) should be deleted. On the grounds of statutory rape I feel that parts (b) (1) and (2) are sufficient reasons for why an abortion may be approved. I can find no reason why the age of a girl should make a difference to allow her to have an abortion.

Furthermore, I find no reason why section 252953 should be laid down. To arbitrarily set the number of physicians and surgeons to be members of "the committee" at a proposed termination of pregnancy is irrational. One "licensed physician and surgeon" is enough to perform an abortion at a proposed termination of pregnancy. Therefore section 252953 should be deleted.

(2) From the last paper you wrote for another course, choose a paragraph which is full of weak verbs. Restructure and rewrite it by using the system described in this chapter. Leave out no steps in the system; do not try to do more than one step at a time; and omit no details from your original paragraph.

Chapter III

WORDS, MEANINGS, AND LABELS

A. DICTIONARIES AND DEFINITIONS

A dictionary definition can tell us for what purposes a word has conventionally been used. It cannot tell us all that may happen to a word when it is placed in a context of other words, nor all that a word might do to the words that surround it. To complicate matters further, contemporary usage constantly is altering the meanings of words, adding new ones, neglecting old ones, selecting new favorites, changing boundaries of definition, and attracting new associations.

Dictionary definitions tell us mainly what a word means in isolation (its denotations). When we know where the word has come from (its etymology), what suggestive and associative shades of meaning it can take upon itself (its connotations), and how users of the word have expanded its possibilities (its metaphoric value), then we have discovered not only what the word can mean, but also what it can do. We presume, and correctly so, that words become defined by conventional use; but we forget that our every use of a word can expand or limit that definition, and that we can define concepts, situations, and relationships through our choice of and use of words. Words affect communication, then, by three major means:

(1) By what they can mean;
(2) By what they can do; and
(3) By how they can be altered.

Words have a symbiotic relationship with the concept they represent. We cannot "know" the meaning of a word without understanding the concept to which it refers. Consider, for example, the distinction between the meanings of the words "sympathy" and "empathy," which are so often misused:

Sympathy   2.c. The quality or state of being thus affected by the suffering or sorrow of another; a feeling of compassion or commiseration. [Examples: "Every expression of human sympathy brings some little comfort." "Sympathy with the bereaved parents and for the bride was deeply felt."]

Empathy   The power of entering into the experience of or understanding objects or emotions outside ourselves. [Examples: "Lipps propounded the theory that the appreciation of a work of art depended upon the capacity of the spectator to project his personality into the object of contemplation. One had to 'feel oneself into it.' This mental process he called by the name of . . . Empathy."—"The active power of empathy which makes the creative artist, or the passive power of empathy which makes the appreciator of art."]

(Oxford English Dictionary) *

They both refer to the process of "feeling along with," but the former is applied to people, while the latter is applied only to objects and emotions. Memorizing this difference will be of no use unless the concepts themselves are understood. These words —indeed, all words—have a symbolic relationship with the thoughts they represent. In fact, words *are* symbols which represent and call to mind those concepts. When we no longer care about a particular thought, the word that stands for it will either die or be put to some other, "incorrect" use. Conversely, when we constantly misuse a word (as we have done for some time now in the case of "empathy"), the thought it refers to will die because we no longer have a way to express it. If we care about our thoughts, we must take extraordinarily good care of our words.

To understand the definition process, then, is to understand a process of thought. The word "define" comes from the Latin

---

* All dictionary definitions used are taken from the *Oxford English Dic-* *tionary* (Oxford: Clarendon Press, 1933).

roots *de,* meaning "about," and *finire,* the verb "to finish" or "to make an end of." "Define," therefore, suggests the making of boundaries that "put an end to" or "limit" an area, in this case an area of thought. In its ideal form, definition would seem to be a rigidifying process, a boundary-drawing that would enclose a set of thoughts or attributes and exclude all others, freezing forever the meaning thus established. In practice, however, we find that we cannot draw those lines clearly enough, nor make them impermeable. All such efforts are foiled by the chameleon and creative nature of words.

Humpty Dumpty said gaily . . . "that shows that there are three hundred and sixty-four days when you might get unbirthday presents—"

"Certainly," said Alice.

"And only *one* for birthday presents, you know. There's glory for you!"

"I don't know what you mean by 'glory,' " Alice said.

Humpty Dumpty smiled contemptuously. "Of course you don't—till I tell you. I meant 'there's a nice knock-down argument for you!' "

"But 'glory' doesn't mean 'a nice knock-down argument,' " Alice objected.

"When *I* use a word," Humpty Dumpty said in a rather scornful tone, "it means just what I choose it to mean —neither more nor less."

"The question is," said Alice, "whether you *can* make words mean so many different things."

"The question is," said Humpty Dumpty, "which is to be master—that's all."

Alice was too much puzzled to say anything, so after a minute Humpty Dumpty began again. "They've a temper, some of them—particularly verbs, they're the proudest—adjectives you can do anything with, but not verbs—however, *I* can manage the whole lot of them! Impenetrability! That's what *I* say!"

"Would you tell me, please," said Alice, "what that means?"

"Now you talk like a reasonable child," said Humpty Dumpty, looking very much pleased. "I meant by 'impenetrability' that we've had enough of that subject, and it would be just as well if you'd mention what you mean to do next, as I suppose you don't mean to stop here all the rest of your life." [1]

Perhaps all the King's soldiers and all the King's men couldn't put Humpty together again because they couldn't follow his directions or respond to his requests. "Congratulate my left leg with might right assurance!" he might have implored. Should they have asked him how he felt, he might have replied, "Abstemious and unforeseeable."

Dumpty could afford his views on language because of his situation in life; but for those of us who do not plan to sit on a wall for the rest of our days, condescending to those who happen along, language must be accepted as a social phenomenon. We must start from some sort of agreement about communication, some set definitional base for the meanings of each word, before we can engage our own imagination and will in our use of language.

If we as a society did not agree that the word "ball" should refer to a spherical object, then it would not; but note that "ball" also refers to a formal social event which involves dancing. One meaning does not negate the other, even though we have a societal "agreement" about each. We seem to have put ourselves in a position of false logic:

First we claim "ball" equals "spherical object," or

$$X = Y$$

Then we claim that "ball" equals "formal dance," or

$$X = Z$$

And yet we cannot claim that a "formal dance" is a "spherical object":

$$X = Y$$
$$X = Z$$
$$Y \neq Z$$

1. Lewis Carroll, *Through the Looking Glass and What Alice Found* *There* (New York: Crown publishers), pp. 123-125.

This is the source of much confusion for foreigners. For example, there is the embarrassed American in Paris who relied too straightforwardly on his dictionary when shopping for antiques. After flipping through the French to English section several times, he bravely asked what he thought was the French equivalent for "How much is that chest of drawers?"—"Combien coute cette poitrine de pantalons?" "Poitrine" does indeed mean chest, but it refers to the upper part of the anatomy, not to furniture. "Pantalons" might well be translated as "drawers," but it would then refer to an article of clothing.

Again, words are merely symbols, recalling for the listener or reader a previously agreed upon concept. Humpty Dumpty suffers from great pride (which went before his fall) in that he uses words asocially, without reference to any previous agreements. If he should do this too often, he might as well be speaking only to himself. Yet his basic inclination is not totally misdirected. We should never consider definitional boundaries unalterable, nor should we think of words as having only one meaning. We are the masters of our language, to a certain extent, but in his totalitarian attitude, Dumpty goes overboard. (We might say nowadays that he is "off the wall.") If we are to maintain our balance and yet not enslave ourselves to the language, we must understand how, why, and when definitional boundaries alter or can be altered.

B.   VARIETIES OF WORD ALTERATIONS

T. S. Eliot warns us:

>   Words strain,
> Crack and sometimes break, under the burden,
> Under the tension, slip, slide, perish,
> Decay with imprecision, will not stay in place,
> Will not stay still.[2]

                           (*Four Quartets*, "Burnt Norton")

The inherent brittleness of words, combined with the fickleness of our use of words, creates a constant frustration for writers.

---

2. T. S. Eliot, "Burnt Norton," *Four Quartets* (New York: Harcourt, Brace, Jovanovich, 1971), V, 149–153, p. 19.

How can we be sure that our words (1) will express all of our thought, (2) will accurately communicate our thought to others, and (3) will remain constant throughout time, even as the language changes? We can be sure of none of these, but we can try to ensure the best odds possible by being critically aware of how and why words can have their meanings altered. The purpose of the following long section on word meanings is to increase awareness of the living qualities of words. Words are the writer's most important tools, and workers at any craft must understand their tools thoroughly before trying to use them professionally.

1. NATURAL MUTATION OF LANGUAGE: CHANGES THROUGH TIME

Instead of inventing new words every time we need a slightly new shade of meaning, we tend to expand definitions of words already in use. As a result, over long periods of time a word can come to be used in a way quite different from its original application. Sometimes the transformations seem inexplicable, as in the case of the word "grey," which now suggests an atmosphere of dullness and depression, but 500 years ago suggested a bright, shining, and rather merry mood.

"Sophisticated" now connotes an air of knowledge, maturity, and complexity, all in a positive sense. If we wish to suggest negative results that could stem from these qualities, we usually speak of "over-sophistication." Originally, however, the word invoked quite a different response. The Sophists were a school of philosophers in ancient Greece who taught their students how to argue either side of any proposition, which often led to the ignoring of the moral issues involved. The skills which that training created were so easily abused that the Sophists fell into bad repute, and their name became the root of a new word that inferred both a complexification of an otherwise simple issue and a process of moral deterioration or adulteration of previous purity. Eventually "sophisticated" came to mean anything that had once been pure and now was spoiled.

"Grey" has fallen from the joyful to the depressed; "sophisticated" has risen from the adulterated to the adulated; but the word "constable" has made both the journey and the return trip.

It has risen from the ignominious, peaked in stardom, and descended once again, coming to rest in ordinary respectability. "Constable" comes from an old two-syllable word "come" (meaning "Count") and "stable." The "Count of the stable" was the young fellow who performed the least noble of tasks, the cleaning of the stables, and the feeding and grooming of the horses. His "title" was conferred in sarcasm. Just as young grooms grow up to take on more respectable and more responsible duties, so did their appellation. "Constable" came to refer to the person in charge of the stables, and then to the person in charge of the purchase and training of the horses (a significant and responsible position in a wealthy household). At length the Army borrowed the term, elevating it again to refer to the person in charge of training the cavalry, and eventually raising it to its greatest glory: for a while, the "Constable" was the cavalry's chief commander, the Generalissimo, the man who made all the important decisions of strategy and discipline for those who fought on horseback. Gradually the term faded out of military life, returned to the civilian scene, and descended in glory until it reached its present dignified but unostentatious level, referring to the position of a minor official in charge of a small precinct within a town.

These changes happen slowly, almost imperceptively. People rarely gather to vote on such issues (although we have seen examples of that recently, as groups have made decisions on the desexing of pronouns, whether to use "he" for male and female instead of "he or she," "she or he," "s/he," or the grammatically improper "they"). Instead, these changes often come about when someone in authority or much in the public eye uses a word with a new shade of meaning, and the people who hear him, her, or them, mimic that use of the word so often that the new meaning becomes grafted to the old. Each of us, then, whether knowingly or not, constantly helps or hinders the process of change in language. Public acceptance or rejection of new words and new meanings will, over time, change the norms of language.

2. SYNTHETIC MUTATION OF LANGUAGE: NEW WORDS; NEW MEANINGS FOR OLD WORDS

Language must keep pace with the needs of society. As we invent new concepts or discover new things we need new terms with which to refer to them. Sometimes the discovery comes first and the naming follows in order that we may use the discovery. Before we knew of the existence of Nitrogen, we had no need for the word; but after we knew of its existence we could not conveniently work with it until it had a name.

Sometimes the name is created first and the referent follows after. Politicians and advertizing moguls take this route on occasion, finding a word or phrase that sounds attractive and building a series of promises or products around it. Normally a basic concept or opportunity (a tight fiscal policy or a new freeze-drying process) precedes the terminology which, in turn, fosters a proliferation of new programs and products.

New words make many people uneasy, however, and as a result we often prefer to expand the meaning of older words instead. One such word which has a remarkably colorful history is "thalamus." Today the term refers to a nucleus in the diencephalon (an area of the brain) which acts as a relay or switching station for different modes of sensory information going to the cerebral cortex (a kind of processing plant for that information). The history of "thalamos," a Greek word, illuminates our choice and use of "thalamus."

Originally it referred to the hold of a ship, the place where the cargo was kept. It also referred to the holes in the side of the ship through which the oars went. (The rowers stationed at the last benches, who therefore had the shortest oars and the lowest pay, were called the Thalamites.) Then it expanded its meaning to include any storehouse for valuable things. Then it contracted to mean the suite of rooms in a large house that belonged to an unmarried son. The rooms were at the center of the structure, thus having no windows and making escape from them most difficult, an excellent "storehouse for valuables." Becoming yet more specific, it then came to signify rooms used as a bridal suite, and a tradition evolved amongst the upper classes to have a poem written expressly for a wedding. They called this poem an "Epithalamion" (literally, "upon the marriage bed"), and its substance dealt with the events of the marriage day and the immortality promised by the fruit of the marriage bed. Thus the root "thalamos" had reached a most specific and narrow application.

Reconsider, then, the function of "Thalamus" to describe the cerebral relay station. The "Thalamus" lies totally within the brain, is concerned with the transmission of a most valuable substance, and is an important part of the proliferation process of mental "offspring" that can outlast its producer. The word, then, is not merely a label; it has become a metaphor.

3. THE DETERIORATION OF LANGUAGE: THE FADING AWAY OF OLD WORDS AND MEANINGS

As "thalamus" changed in meaning it continued to grow and maintain its vitality and usefulness. More often, unfortunately, in this verbally lazy age of ours, words deteriorate over time and thereby erode our abilities to make fine distinctions in feeling and thought. We have seen a great deal of this in the past few decades, as the excesses and shocks of modern life makes it harder and harder for us to feel shocked or awed by anything.

The overuse of the superlative both exemplifies and symbolizes this process. The superlative, formed by adding "most" or "-est" to a modifier, should communicate a sense of "to the greatest extent possible," and should be reserved for those rare occasions when we encounter true extremities in life. Today, however, we see almost every product or experience advertised as "the most" or "the _____est" of its kind, and it requires a fresh kind of wit to restore to us our sense of "superlative."

In the same way, words that used to convey extreme emotional reactions now mean little more than "good" or "O.K." or "darn." Consider the following uses of a word that once meant "that which terrifies":

"How'd ya like the show?"
"It was terrific. I laughed all the way through it."

"I can meet you downtown tomorrow at Noon."
"Terrific. See you then."

"The car broke down today, so I took it to the repair shop."
"O terrific! Now I'll have to take the train instead, and I'll be late to work."

"Wonderful" now means no more than "terrific" does; it used to mean "full of wonder." "Awful" used to mean "that which inspires one with awe," and it was used to describe cathedrals and holy ceremonies. Nowadays the only thing called "awful" in a church is an occasional sermon, and then only when it has inspired sleep, not awe. "Fantastic" used to mean "that which can only be imagined in fantasy" or "that which has the qualities of fantasy, as opposed to reality"; now it too means "O.K." or "good." "Horrible" used to mean "that which can inspire one with horror"; now it means "not up to par," and it describes a bad movie or a poorly played game of golf.

This process of overuse and careless use transforms formerly descriptive words and phrases into "clichés," catchwords with hollow reverberations, sound with little sense. Recent examples include "meaningful experience," "generation gap," and "nervous breakdown," none of which mean anywhere near as much as they once did. We are in danger of losing altogether the usefulness of "significant," "relevant," "substantial," "really," and "interesting." "Unique" and "crucial" are losing their sense of extremity, as scores of television ads claim "uniqueness" for their products, and sportscasters hype every other game as a "crucial" match.

Other words lose their former effectiveness when a new meaning overshadows older ones. "Amateur" (from the Latin verb *amare*, "to love") used to signify one who did something out of the love of doing it; then it became merely the opposite of "professional" (one who is paid for doing it); and now it suggests a kind of incompetency, inferring cynically that one cannot be good at anything unless one is paid for it. Such a change would be of little consequence if we had some other word to refer in a positive sense to someone who does things for the love of it. Having no such word, we begin to lose the concept itself; as a result, fewer people participate and more people spectate. Another indication of the relationship between the word change and the thought change is that precisely the same fate has befallen the word "dilletante" (from the Italian *diletto,* "to take delight in").

A "chauvanist" used to be one who was completely committed to a cause or an identity, a "My country, right or wrong" kind of person. In the reaction against the concept of Nationalism, "chauvanist" came to signify a person unthinkingly devoted to a single cause. With the struggle of women to claim equal recognition, the word, as a shorthand for "male chauvanist pig," has become unmitigatedly negative, referring to a perpetrator of conscious and unconscious prejudices. Once again, the original meaning has faded away along with the concept that supported it, although we still have words like "patriot" and phrases like "a loyal _____" to replace it. If these loyalties were to die away, the words would disappear with them, just as the technical terms for repairing horse-drawn vehicles have vanished. A list of them would mystify most of us.

4. THE INFLUENCE OF FOREIGN LANGUAGES

Foreign words enter a language either by imposition (see Chapter I, Part D) or through assimilation (when one country apes another's manners, fashions, or technology). While the kind of political and social traumae that produce the former happen only occasionally, the latter kind of semantic infiltration continues steadily.

When we admire another country's prowess in a certain area, we are as quick to import their terminology as we are their products. We use the French term "chic" because we have for so long looked to Paris for the lead in fashion-designing. Our use of "fiancé(e)" might be a tribute to the legendary French supremacy in matters of the heart. In turn, the French declare their approval of the Anglo-American sweater by adopting the term as *le sweater* (accenting the final syllable) and for the British riding coat by creating *la redingote.* The British, ironically, copied the copy, apparently forgetting it had been theirs to start with, and now sell a garment called a "redingote" in England.

Such borrowings may keep the original meanings intact or may change them radically, depending on the needs and understanding of the borrowing country. Eventually the word becomes "accepted" into the adopting language, and the foreignness becomes only a part of its etymology.

5. COINAGE, INTENTIONAL AND ACCIDENTAL

Sometimes a public person either knowingly or through ignorance invents a word which remains part of the language. In some cases people simply like the word and wish to retain it; in other cases they assume the public person would not make such a mistake and that the word had long been a part of the language. We have no reliable statistics about such things, but the all-time leader in successful coinage seems to be Shakespeare. Most writers use a vocabulary of from 7,000 to 12,000 words; Shakespeare used 25,000 words, many of which he invented, and it is a tribute to his ingenuity and mastery that any writer today can claim legitimacy for a word simply by demonstrating that Shakespeare had used it several centuries earlier.

The advertizing industry plays games with the language at times when it tries to produce memorable slogans that will entice consumers to purchase its product. Most of these clever concoctions disappear quickly, as was the case in the attempt to make a particular toilet tissue seem both "strong" and "soft" by calling it "stroft." The word has not taken hold in the language, perhaps because that product has yet to corner the market in toilet tissue.

On occasion a commercial success has transformed a brand name into a new English word. "Xerox" can now refer to the electronic copying process, no matter what brand machine is involved. We have learned to use "scotch tape," even if it is not "Scotch Tape," and no sneezers will be refused a tissue if they ask for a "Kleenex" and the potential donor only has some other brand at the moment. It is even possible for a brand name to have become so "generic" that the original company will be denied exclusive use of the words.

The greatest honor for a brand name is for it to undergo a metamorphosis into a metaphor. Cadillac, for example, has so long been the symbol of American automotive luxury that General Motors can advertize that to call anything "Cadillac" is to call it the best of its kind. When success is associated with a name for a long enough period of time, the name, in turn, can breed more successes.

Political figures and others who appear regularly in the mass media provide us with the majority of our accidental coinages. Sometimes it seems that the public will continue to use some famous malapropism (like the word "normalcy," unknowingly coined by President Harding) in order to lessen the coiner's embarrassment, just as a proper hostess will spill her wine intentionally to lessen the dismay of a guest who has just spilled his.

6. INFORMAL LANGUAGE: SLANG

Sometimes instead of adding an extra definition to fit a given word, we add an extra word to a given definition. When the new word does not supercede the old but rather replaces it only in situations which call for less formal language, the new word falls into the category of slang. While the slang word refers to the same thing, act, or thought as the formal word, it communicates a different attitude on the part of the speaker. Slang can serve a number of different purposes.

(a) Slang often deformalizes, thereby deemphasizing the seriousness of a situation. Thus, to ease the anxiety of his friends and relatives who come to visit him in the hospital, a heart attack patient might lightly refer to his "bad ticker" rather than discuss his "heart problems" or (more frightening still) his "cardiac condition."

(b) Conversely, slang can captivate attention when its root meaning far outweighs in seriousness the nature of the situation to which it refers. Thus sportscasters sometimes nickname a young ballclub that tends to leave its fans in doubt until the last minutes of the game "the cardiac kids."

(c) In a similar way, slang can dramatize situations through metaphoric reference. For example, since sporting events often engage two teams in a struggle against each other, sportscasters have come to use a great deal of war terminology to describe the action on the field or the court. The game becomes a "conflict" or a "battle." In baseball, strike-out "kings" "gun down" the opposing "troops," and teams which lose by lopsided scores are said to have been "killed" that day. In football one of the most exciting plays is "the long bomb," a long pass which descends in the manner of a bomb and usually leads to explosive action upon arrival.

(d) Slang offers endless sources of variety, since it can be created by anyone who has a large enough audience to receive it. When newsmen tire of referring to Congressmen, they call them "lawmakers" (a descriptive term) or "solons" (a slang term, referring to Solon, the wisest man of his day in Ancient Greece). A good many slang words and contractions have developed simply from the limitation of space in newspaper headlines ("Reps" for members of the House of Representatives or "Mob" for organized crime).

(e) Occasionally lazy pronunciation of a long word or phrase will give birth to a new spelling that transliterates the sound and creates a new word. (Whether or not this technically constitutes slang, the word-creating process is the same.) The British have a fondness for this metamorphosis. Centuries ago they created the word "bedlam," meaning "like a madhouse" from their abbreviation of the pronunciation of Bethlehem, the name of the major madhouse of London. They did the same with the name of Mary Magdalene (which they pronounced "Mary Mod-lin"), creating a new word, "maudlin," to describe the mood of someone who, like Mary Magdalene, is always found weeping. Perhaps the most outlandish example of British spelling ingenuity is "Elephant and Castle" (now one of the stops on the London underground rail transportation system). That place was the site of festivities when the heir to the throne of Castile (in Spain) paid a visit to England several hundred years ago. His title, "L'Enfant de Castile", was mangled into the English "Elephant and Castle," and so it remains.

(g) Beyond its dramatic and convenience functions, slang is often created as a method of expressing identity, either for an established group of people or for an activity done by a revolving group of people. Ethnic groups are often examples of the former, developing a vocabulary which makes them distinctive from all other groups. (Indeed, while the new words are classified as slang for the rest of the public, the group that creates them would look upon them as basic and normative.)

The recreational and entertainment businesses provide many examples of the other type. An uninitiated visitor to Las Vegas might take the game of Blackjack to be a sado-masochistic activity, as each player in turn requests the dealer to "hit me." Language of this sort binds together the people who understand it and excludes everyone else. The same function is performed by codes, passwords, and secret handshakes.

C. ETYMOLOGIES

We have seen that words change through time, gaining, losing, and exchanging meanings. Etymology is the branch of linguistics that studies the derivation of words. An individual etymology traces the origin and development of a single word much in the same way that a genealogy traces the history of a family. Spending time with etymologies can transform your perception of what words are and make you more conscious of their living (and dying) qualities. At the same time, it can be most entertaining. The delight they produce is due to the joy of discovery, especially that particular feeling of surprise when we see something new in a familiar old sight. Since paying attention to etymologies can help you develop new sensitivities to words and how they connect thought and expression, we shall take a look at a good many of them.

1. WORDS NAMED AFTER PEOPLE, PLACES, AND THINGS

nicotine   Named after Jean Nicot, ambassador of France at Lisbon, who first introduced tobacco into France (1560).

poinsettia   Named after Joel Roberts Poinsett (1779–1851), American minister to Mexico, discoverer of the plant.

lynch   Named after Captain William Lynch of Pittsylvania, Virginia, who first set up a self-created judicial tribunal in America.

lady bug   Most people feel it is "bad luck" to kill one of these orange and black insects, and most know the old rhyme, "Lady bug, lady bug, fly away home,/Your house is on fire, your children will burn." The reason for both of these is that the bug gets its name from being associated with the Virgin Mary, literally "the bug of Our Lady." If you want to get rid of one of these, then, you must lie to it, pretending its house to be afire, since respect for the Virgin prevents you from harming it.

tawdry   Short for "tawdry laces," a cheap kind of ornament to be worn around the neck; the word recalls St. Audrey, patron saint of Ely in England, who died from a throat tumor, just retribution, she thought, for her youthful fondness for decorative necklaces. An annual St. Audrey's Fair is held at Ely every October 17, where one may buy "t'Audrey laces."

monetary   Named after the queen of the Roman goddesses, Juno, sometimes called Juno Moneta (literally "Juno who warns or admonishes"). Perhaps because she was considered the most serious of the goddesses, all minting of money was done at her shrines, thus transforming "Moneta" into our "monetary," "mint," and "money."

masochist   Meaning someone who takes sexual pleasure in being hurt, the word celebrates Leopold Sacher Masoch (1836-1895), who describes it in his novels.

sadist   The converse of masochist, the sadist takes pleasure in hurting others, and owes his title to the Marquis de Sade (1740-1814), who describes the process in his novels.

hoodlum   Coined by a San Francisco journalist (19th Century); a reversal of the spelling of Muldoon, the leader of a gang of young ruffians. A typographical error by the compositor substituted an "h" for the "n."

thug   The name of a group of professional robbers and murderers in India.

assassin   From "hasshah," "eater of hashish"; it refers to Moslem fanatics who were paid to murder Christians.

They found the task easier to accomplish if they intoxicated themselves with hashish beforehand.

tycoon   Foreigners' title for the Shogun of Japan during the 19th Century: *ta* ("great") + *kiun* ("prince").

lush   After the "city of Lushington," a convivial society which met at the Harp Tavern, Russell Street, London, until 1895.

tuxedo   Reflects the fancy dress often worn at Tuxedo Park, an exclusive country club at Tuxedo Lake, New York. The word was originally a corruption of *p'tuksit*, a North American Indian dialect name for the wolf.

Monday   The day of the Moon (cf. French *lundi* after the French word *lune*, meaning "moon").

Tuesday   Tyr's day; Tyr was the Teutonic equivalent of the god mars (cf. French *mardi*).

Wednesday   Odin's day. The Roman god Mercury is often associated with the Teutonic god Odin (cf. French *mercredi*).

Thursday   Thor's day. The Roman god Jove is often associated with the Teutonic god Thor (cf. French *jeudi*).

Friday   Frigg's day. The Roman goddess Venus is often associated with the Teutonic goddess Frigg (cf. French *vendredi*).

Saturday   Saturn's day, Saturn being a pre-Jove Roman god. (The French term is *samedi*, probably coming from Latin words for "seventh" and "sabbath." In the Jewish week, Saturday is the sabbath.)

Sunday   The day of the Sun. (The French use *dimanche*, from *s'endimancher*, "to dress in one's best," which may come from the Latin *dies dominicus*, "day of the lord.")

2. WORDS GENERATED BY TRADITIONAL ACTIONS

sabotage   From the Dutch *sabot*, "wooden shoes," which were thrown into machinery to stop factories' production.

fornicate	From the Latin *fornus*, "archway"; in Roman times prostitutes were known to lurk under certain archways in the city.
hangar	From the Old High German word meaning "to hang"; a place where horses were suspended for the purpose of being shod.
handicap	In a dispute over ownership of property, the parties concerned would put their forfeits into a hat, and an impartial umpire would put his "hand in the cap" to draw out the winner.
ballot	In 16th Century Venice one voted by dropping a small ball into the appropriate box.
lord	From the Old English *hlaf* ("bread") and *weard* ("protector"); *hlaf-weard* contracted to "lord."
lady	From the Old English *hlaf* ("bread") and *dige* ("one who kneads").
-ster	A suffix indicating a doer of an action: cf. songster, youngster, gangster, seamster, tapster, gamester, spinster, trickster, rhymester, roadster, and punster. It is found also in family names: Websters once wove, Baxters once baked, and Brewsters once brewed.

3. WORDS WHICH INDICATE A FUNCTION

sheriff	The "reve" of a "shire," "reve" being a municipal officer and "shire" being the British equivalent of the American "county."
fine	From the Latin *finis*, meaning "end"; in the legal sense a fine was an amount of money paid to put an end to a judicial proceeding.
verdict	From the latin *veritas* ("truth") and *dicere* ("to say"); a "verdict" was not simply the final outcome of a trial, but rather the pronouncing of the truth of the case.
abatement	From Latin and French, meaning literally "a beating down."
alto	From the Latin *altus*, meaning "high"; although today the alto part is sung by the lowest female

voice, it used to be the highest of the men's parts, the soprano being sung by boys, and women being excluded altogether.

clap-trap An English invention: literally a cheap antic on stage with which one might trap a clap, that is, encourage applause.

4. PLACE-NAMES

Vermont Green mountain.

Milford A ford of the river where a mill was built.

Oxford A ford of the river where it was possible to let the oxen cross.

Brooklyn An area delineated by the line of a brook.

Newton A new town.

Cambridge The place where a bridge was built over the River Cam.

Medford A spot at the middle of a river for a ford.

Belmont Beautiful mountain.

Louisville Town built to honor Louis.

5. WORDS FORMED FROM THE ABBREVIATION OF OR COMBINATION OF OTHER WORDS

goon A "portmanteau word," combining two other words, "gorilla" and "baboon"; (cf. "chortle," a combination of "chuckle" and "snort").

Abecedarian A young scholar engaged in learning the ABC's.

lackadaisical A melancholic and slothful person who continually laments, "Alack the day I was born."

umpire A non-peer; through careless pronunciation "a non-peer" became "an umpire."

tweed Trade name originated by a misreading of twilled wool (perhaps in association with the Tweed River in Scotland).

jeep A General Purpose vehicle in the army, nicknamed GP and pronounced (then spelled) "jeep."

tip
: 19th Century sign next to plate for gratuities in english pubs; *To Insure Promptness.*

curfew
: From the French *couvre* ("cover") and *feu* ("fire"); to prevent conflagrations started from home fires negligently left to burn after the family had gone to sleep, towns in France used to prohibit all fires after a certain point of the evening, marked by the ringing of a bell. When the bell rang, residents would have to "cover their fires."

vinegar
: From the French *vin* ("wine") and *aigre* ("sour"), and therefore directly descriptive of the process by which vinegar is produced.

dandelion
: From the French *dents de lion* ("teeth of the lion"); presumably descriptive of the shape of the petals.

6.   WORDS CREATED BY WIT AND WHIMSY

quiz
: In 1780, one Daley, manager of a Dublin theatre, wagered that singlehandedly he could introduce a new word into the English language. To win his bet, he posted signs all around Dublin displaying his creation, "quiz," (a highly unlikely combination of letters, "q" and "z" being two of the least used letters in the language). Apparently few people were willing to admit they had never seen the word before, although everyone questioned what the signs were trying to advertize. As a result, the word became associated with asking questions.

absquatulate
: An intentionally pretentious Americanism, combining the Latin prefix *ab* ("away from"), the Latinate suffix *-ulate* (indicating an action performed), and the American slang term "squat" (to take possession of land by settling on it instead of by acquiring title to it). "Absquatulate," therefore, means to decamp, to cease squatting in one place for the purposes of squatting elsewhere.

serendipity
: Coined in 1754 by Walpole for his fairy tale "The Three Princes of Serendip," the heroes of which

were always making the most agreeably fortuitous discoveries. The term describes the faculty or ability of making such discoveries.

pedigree   From the French *pied de grue* ("foot of the crane"). Family trees usually show a branching pattern with horizontal lines underlining the proper names and vertical lines connecting them to their progeny. The footprint of a crane also shows several nearly vertical lines emanating from a horizontal one— ⌒⊓⌒ —, and therefore a family tree, from a distance, looks like a piece of paper that has been much walked on by a crane. It is of especial interest that a term with such serious and prestigious connotations should actually have as its history a rather low form of humor.

EXERCISE

The following is a list of words that have interesting histories. Search out any thirty of them in any substantial etymological dictionary, a selection of which should be in any good library. Then browse through the dictionary and find ten more of interest that do not appear on this list.

aardvark	boss	handsome cab	May	sinister
abhominable	boycott	hazzard	meticulous	snob
acorn	casino	infant	monarch	sophisticated
acre	cobalt	janitor	nickname	tandem
adjourn	daisy	January	November	tangerine
adroit	December	July	October	tattoo (bugle call)
affront	dizzy	juror	omelet	taxi
agony	dunce	khaki	opera	telephone
alderman	eleven	knickerbocker	paunch	tennis
alibi	elite	lace	pavan	tenor
ambition	fashion	landslide	pen	ulterior
ammonia	February	lethal	perfume	umbrage
anecdote	felon	liaison	prestige	umbrella
animal	flabbergast	linoleum	Quaker	venom
April	fricassee	loco	quarantine	vodka
apron	gale	lounge	ragout	Welsh rarebit
August	gauche	love (tennis)	rake	xenophobic
bandanna	gerrymander	lunatic	scallion	xylophone
banquet	graple	magazine	school (of fish)	yahoo
barrister	gregarious	maim	September	yokel
beserk	gymnastics	March	shambles	zip
bisquit	handsome	marshall	silly	zoo

D. LABELS

The Protean character of words necessitates that we exercise strong, wakeful control over the ones we use, both defensively, to guard against words having their own way in our sentences, and offensively, to control the reader's response insofar as we can. Before we can direct a reader's thought process, we must learn to control the words we use, for words act as labels to our thoughts.

Fan Tchai asked Kung the master (viz Confucius) for instruction in farming. Said the Master: I know less than any old peasant. He made the same reply about gardening: Any old gardner knows more than I do.

Tseu-Leu asked: If the Prince of Mei appointed you head of the government, to what would you first set your mind?

KUNG: To call people and things by their names, that is by the correct denominations, to see that the terminology was exact.

"You mean that is the first?" said Tseu-Leu. "Aren't you dodging the question? What's the use of that?"

KUNG: You are a blank. An intelligent man hesitates to talk of what he don't understand, he feels embarrassment.

If the terminology be not exact, if it fit not the thing, the governmental instructions will not be explicit, if the instructions aren't clear and the names don't fit, you cannot conduct business properly.

If business is not properly run the rites and music will not be honoured, if the rites and music be not honoured, penalties and punishments will not achieve their intended effects, if penalties and punishments do not produce equity and justice, the people won't know where to put their feet or what to lay hold of or to whom they should stretch out their hands.

That is why an intelligent man cares for his terminology and given instructions that fit. When his orders are clear and explicit they can be put into effect. An intelligent man is neither inconsiderate of others nor futile in his command-ing.[3]

(Ezra Pound, *Guide to Kulchur*)

Through our ability to label or to name we achieve the power to create, the god-like power to produce something from nothing. This differs from the acts of discovering and inventing, in which we rearrange materials and concepts already in existence. Creation is almost a magical power, rarely in the grasp of humans and never, we believe, in the grasp of animal or plant life.

When your cat has a litter of kittens, we cannot say she "created" them, since they hardly were produced out of "nothing"; but when you carefully inspect the five kittens, noticing that all have spots except for the one that is solid black, and you ceremoniously proclaim that the black one shall be known as "Spot," you are creating something. Out of nothing you have brought to life a name, a label, the beginning of a personality, a directive for other's response. Nothing of "Spot-ness" would have existed for the black kitten had you not created it; only the potential for "Spot-ness" would have been there.

So it was in the creation story in *Genesis*. God is not pictured producing "light" with His hands or His mind. "Let there be light, and there was light." The naming of light called it into creation. Its potential had always existed (God being God), but only through the labeling process did it materialize. In *Genesis* God gives formal names to only five things (Day, Night, Heaven, Earth, Seas), after which He turns over the task to Adam, who names all the animals, giving Man a further superiority over the rest of life. Adam actually takes part in the creation of "elephant" by choosing the name. Had he called it "gazelle" instead, something (although it is difficult to articulate exactly what) would have been different in our response to the animal.

Consider carefully the following examples of labeling or naming. Before reading on, try to discern in each case what was being created, how important it was, and why it might succeed or fail in

---

3. Ezra Pound, *Guide to Kulchur*
(New York: New Directors, 1968),
pp. 16–17.

its purpose. Thoughts and questions about each example will follow.

(a) The Federal Government changed the name of the Commission on the Aged to the Commission on the Aging.

(b) A President withheld legislation granting tax rebates to the very poor until he could think of a title for the Act more positive than "Negative Income Tax."

(c) A television sports network decided to eliminate the term "sudden death" (referring to the ending of a deadlocked game by the first score in an overtime period) and to use "sudden victory" instead.

(d) As part of combat training, soldiers were taught to refer to the Vietnamese enemy as "Gooks."

(e) At the end of a war, a country changed the name of the Department of War to the Department of Defense, without making any alterations in the Department's proscribed functions.

(f) A Sociologist filed a bill in the State Senate to substitute the term "Rehabilitation Center" for "Jail" and "Penitentiary" throughout the state.

(g) A manufacturer of razors and razor blades announced its newest creation, the "Bonded Shaving System" (which was nothing more than a razor with a razor blade fixed within it), proclaiming it to be set to "the precise shaving angle."

In each case the people or institutions wishing to make the changes seemed to place great faith in the effects of labeling. All the richest and most powerful forces in our society concur: Government consults with highly paid "experts" before naming an agency or a program; the advertising media seem to think of little else; merchants know that a good product with a weak name will not sell as well as a mediocre product with an appealing name; and authors know that many a book, contrary to the adage, is indeed known by its cover. The power to label is a power to create, a power to control. It is a primary example of what words can do (as opposed to what they can mean).

Returning to the examples above, here are several thoughts and questions about each.

(a) The Federal Government changed the name of the Commission on the Aged to the Commission on the Aging.

—The Government apparently felt that older people would respond better to being called "aging" than "aged." Why?

—Does "aged" imply two classes of people, the "aged" and the "not yet aged"?

—Is not every person, even the most newly born, "aging"?

—Does the term "aging" destroy "class distinctions" so thoroughly that it becomes meaningless?

—Does the population as a whole think of the "aging" differently than they think of the "aged"? Do we even recognize a group known as the "aging"?

—Has the Government merely replaced one descriptive term with another, or has it fundamentally altered our perceptions and attitudes?

—The term has been around for several years now; how familiar is it to you? Has it "caught on"?

(b) A President withheld legislation granting tax rebates to the very poor until he could think of a title for the Act more positive than "Negative Income Tax."

—What do you imagine the President thought was wrong with the term "Negative Income Tax"?

—How would you feel about it if you were one of the recipients?

—Is the term so significantly harmful that it was worthwhile delaying the initiation of the legislation to find another label for the same relief?

—In this case would you call the fear of negative labeling sensitivity? paranoia? something in between?

—Was the President worried about the public's confusing the operative meaning of "negative" ("less than zero") with its stronger but inappropriate meaning ("not positive in attitude")? Why? Would it have had any effect on his next campaign for re-election?

(c) A television sports network decided to eliminate the term "sudden death" (referring to the ending of a deadlocked game by the first score in an overtime period) and to use "sudden victory" instead.

—From where do you suppose the pressure came that made the network attempt to change the terminology?

—Which term is more dramatic? Why?

—Which term better describes the situation? Why?

—The term did not catch on, especially because the sportscasters could not seem to become comfortable with it. Why should they have had so much trouble? Were they just too accustomed to the old term, or is there something generically false about "sudden victory"?

—Does death normally come "suddenly"? Does it ever come any other way, and if so, how?

—Does victory normally come "suddenly"? Does it ever come any other way?

—How much control do people have over the coming of death? Over the coming of victory? What does "sudden" have to do with the concept of control?

—Which term pleases better in terms of mere sound? Which sound more closely approximates the process referred to by the terms?

—Should we be more interested in victory than death? Is either more "civilized" than the other? Was this part of the network's reasoning?

—Is either term more realistic than the other?

—In a sports event, what should the relationship between "civilization" and "reality" be?

(d) As part of combat training, soldiers were taught to refer to the Vietnamese enemy as "Gooks."

—There is an inherent moral problem in teaching young men to obey orders and to break one of the Ten Commandments simultaneously; how does renaming the enemy help solve this problem?

—Giving inanimate objects human names often gives them personality (e.g., calling the family car "Sally"); does giving a human an inanimate label decrease the person's humanity?

—Is it morally easier to kill a "Gook" than to kill a "Vietnamese"? or a "Nguen"? or a "Theodore"? Why?

—Is it easier to kill a member of a group than an individual?

(e) At the end of a war, a country changed the name of the Department of War to the Department of Defense, without making any alterations in the Department's proscribed functions.

—For whose benefit was the name changed?

—Might the change affect the attitudes of the people who work for the Department, even if their tasks remain the same?

—How would the country's allies respond to the change? How would its enemies respond? Would it make any real difference to another country nowadays?

—What else might the country have to change as a result of exchanging "War" for "Defense"?

—After twenty years had passed, and the war is relegated to "history," would the change in label then be more likely to affect the function and purpose of the Department?

(f) A Sociologist filed a bill in the State Senate to substitute the term "Rehabilitation Center" for "Jail" and "Penitentiary" throughout the state.

—What will the term "rehabilitation" allow the prison authorities to do that they cannot do now?

—What does "rehabilitation" mean, and from what root does it come? Has the etymology anything to do with the effect of the word?

—Is this a case of merely substituting one descriptive term for another? Does the label have a positive effect? Does it have an evasive effect?

—Can "rehabilitation" take place at a jail if it continues to be called "Jail"? Will it actually be easier to rehabilitate prisoners if the name is changed to "Rehabilitation Center"?

—What positive effects could the name change have on the prisoners? What negative effects?

—Why is a Sociologist asking for the change? Would it make a difference if someone else were doing the asking (e.g., a prisoner, a prisoner's association, the warden, the newspapers, a public interest group)?

(g) A manufacturer of razors and razor blades announced its newest creation, the "Bonded Shaving System," (which was nothing more than a razor with a razor blade fixed within it), proclaiming it to be set to "the precise shaving angle."

—What can a "bonded shaving system" do that a regular razor and blade cannot? What does it imply it can do?

—Which words identify this ad as a product of the 20th Century?

—What kind of confidence does the word "bonded" inspire, and from where does that confidence come?

—What impression does the word "system" make and why?

—What about the normal use of a razor makes a "bonded system" sound particularly attractive?

—What is "the precise shaving angle"? How does it support the claims of the razor being a "bonded shaving system."?

—How does this "precise" angle help this razor to compete against the best-selling razor that "adjusts to nine different angles to suit any face"? According to the "precise angle" company, are nine angles better or worse than one?

The Chinese have long told us that one picture is worth a thousand words. Madison Avenue now tells us that the right word is worth a thousand words. Since the advertising agencies understand the complex human response to the stimulus of a printed word (and since most readers of advertisements do not), manufacturers can, with the right ad agency and the right combination of words, manipulate the public into believing in the superiority of their product over an equally functional and sound competing product. Shampoo producers would have us "love" our hair, "care" for it, and "condition" it. If they merely urged us to "wash" it and promised it would be "clean" and "unharmed" by their product, we would feel no devotion, no moral pleasure, no sense of health and guardianship in the constant attention we pay to it, and we would not buy their product, or not buy as much of it. "Love" implies a moral commitment; "care" suggests a sense of maturity and responsibility; "condition" raises in our minds a notion of health and sexual attractiveness. "Cleanliness" and "washing," on the other hand, remind us more of Victorian Nanny figures in starched collars, demanding obedience of children who would prefer to avoid the subject altogether.

The public can even be convinced to buy products that do not measure up to the standards of quality which that same public has previously decided are essential. Two striking examples come to mind in particular. In the 1950's clothing manufacturers decided to invest in a fabric from India known as Madras. It was most colorful and came in bright combinations of stripes and plaids, and its light weight made it ideal for wear in the warmest of weather. One characteristic of the cloth seemed to doom it, however; the material would bleed uncontrollably when washed, and the Bermuda shorts or the summer shirt would appear shabby, old, and faded a week after purchase. Madison Avenue came to the rescue, with the result that Madras dominated the market for years: On every garment appeared a tag proclaiming, "Genuine Madras—guaranteed to bleed." Not only did Madras always live up to its guarantee, but all your neighbors could recognize that you were wearing "the real thing" because of its shabby, old, faded appearance.

An Alaskan fish company tried to sell a special salmon indigenous to a small area of the Western shores of that state. Unfortunately its color was a pinkish white, instead of the pinkish mauve of most salmon, and the public shied away from the product because it looked anemic. The company solved that problem by a Madrasian promise printed on every tin: "This salmon guaranteed not to turn pink in the can."

EXERCISES

Comment as thoroughly as possible on the effects of the following word choices.

(1) A company that makes orange juice from concentrate prints on each package "100% pure."

(2) A candidate for a state judgeship advertises himself as being strongly supportive of "law and order."

(3) A veterinarian informs the owner of a dog that the animal will have to be "put to sleep."

(4) In trying to convince her husband to purchase a new, extremely expensive house, a wife argues that it would be more than a "home"; it would be a "family living center."

(5) A state agency decides that in the future all autistic and retarded children will be referred to as "exceptional children."

(6) A restaurant tries to decide what sign to put on the doors of the rooms that contain toilets and sinks for the use of its patrons. What are the messages communicated by each of the following possibilities, and what would the restaurant be saying about itself in each case?

(a) Gentlemen/Ladies

(b) Men/Women

(c) Rest room

(d) Bathroom

(e) Toilet

(f) The Loo

(g) W.C.

(h) The Head

(i) Powder Room

Chapter IV

DEFINITIONAL BOUNDARIES: THE PROBLEMS OF CONTROL

A. MUTATION OF MEANING THROUGH CONTEXT: DENOTATION AND CONNOTATION

We have defined "word" as a group of letters which, taken as a symbol, communicates a series of agreed upon meanings. At the core of this definition lies the concept of agreement. If we intend to communicate with others, we cannot adopt the attitude of Humpty Dumpty, who made words mean whatever he wished whenever he wished.

Although it is difficult to pin down exactly who are the arbiters of word acceptance in a language, the public more or less turns to dictionaries as the authoritative source of information on the subject. The meanings to be found there constitute the word's denotations, the meanings that we as a society have decided to attach to that particular word. We distinguish denotations (explicit meanings) from connotations, which the *Oxford English Dictionary* defines as "The signifying in addition; inclusion of something in the meaning of a word besides that which it primarily denotes; implication." In a sense, denotation tells us how a word can be used, while connotation tells us when and in what circumstances it should be used. "Bathroom" and "Powder Room" both refer to the same denotative concept, but the connotation of the former forbids its use in the social situations for which "Powder Room" would be appropriate, and vice versa.

Societal agreement is crucial for the creating and limiting of meaning for both denotation and connotation; but an unagreed upon denotative use will normally lead to the comment being unintelligible, whereas an unagreed upon connotative use will more likely lead to the embarrassment of the speaker.

74

The same concept of agreement has led to the establishment of norms for spelling, punctuation, paragraphing, and other structural and grammatical conventions. No single principle makes the spelling of words consistent. We no longer hallow the past by maintaining etymological traces of word development; we have excised some of the "useless" letters (like the British "u" in vigour /vigor); we have tried to make concessions to the exigencies of space, which is neither plentiful nor inexpensive ("Thruway" for "Thoroughway"); and we allow alternate spellings when agreement on one cannot be reached ("traveled" and "travelled" are both considered correct). Yet despite all this, we are still saddled with a language that is spelled in a way it no longer sounds. George Bernard Shaw went out of his way to dramatize the situation by suggesting that the letter-combination "ghoti" ought to be pronounced fish, considering the way we spell several other words in the language:

"gh" = [f], as in "rough"

"o" = [i], as in "women"

"ti" = [sh], as in "nation"

"Ghoti" = [fish].

Spelling attained stability only with the advent of dictionaries in the Eighteenth Century. Before then people tended to spell words either by the way they sounded or by the way someone else had spelled them previously. Imagine the confusion of the Seventeenth Century Londoners trying to make sense out of Captain John Smith's description of a new animal he had seen in America, variously presented as the "rahaugcum," the "raugroughsum," the "aroughcum," and the "rarowcum." He was referring to the raccoon.

If such are the difficulties inherent in something as harmlessly conventional as spelling, then non-agreement concerning denotative meaning in words should cause complete havoc. As we have seen, words change over time and through contextual change, and they thus develop many shades of meanings, gaining many more than they lose over time. Most of the words that fade away completely do so because their function has faded before them (e.g., parts for machines that are no longer in use, or fashions that have had their day).

Denotation tends towards the process of definition (limiting the boundaries of a concept), while connotation tends towards the process of description (communicating the impressionistic essence of a concept or experience). Without a strong sense of both, a reader cannot understand the thoughts that have prompted the writer to write. Treating denotation without care will lead to a general imprecision in language, which eventually will lead to a general decay in communication. Disregarding connotation, however, leads to an isolation from human experience and a lack of understanding of the emotional essence of things.

In his novel *Hard Times*, Charles Dickens pits a champion of denotation, Thomas Gradgrind, a schoolmaster interested only in "facts," against a young girl who understands the essence of things, what they connote, but has not the weapons of definitional exactitude with which to defend herself.

" .   .   Give me your definition of a horse."

(Sissy Jupe thrown into the greatest alarm by this demand.)

"Girl number twenty unable to define a horse!" said Mr. Gradgrind, for the general behoof of all the little pitchers. "Girl number twenty possessed of no facts in reference to one of the commonest of animals! Some boy's definition of a horse. Bitzer, yours."

"Quadruped. Graminivorous. Forty teeth, namely twenty-four grinders, four eye-teeth, and twelve incisive. Sheds coat in the spring; in marshy countries, sheds hoofs, too. Hoofs hard, but requiring to be shod with iron. Age known by marks in the mouth." Thus (and much more) Bitzer.

"Now, girl number twenty," said Mr. Gradgrind, "you know what a horse is."[1]

Sissy Jupe had spent all her young life in the company of a travelling circus, to which she refers as "the horse-riding." She understands "what a horse is" in a way different (and probably more intense, more intimate) from the understanding that Mr. Gradgrind has; and yet we cannot say he is unjustified in his

1. Charles Dickens, *Hard Times* (London: Bradbury & Evans, 1854), pp. 6–7.

search for denotative knowledge. Certainly both are necessary in the practice of the Law, which requires both precision and intuition.

Gradgrind suggests that Sissy should be ashamed for not knowing the definition of "one of the commonest of animals." You have probably seen horses, at least on movie and television screens, but perhaps in person as well. What kind of knowledge do you have about them? When you see the word, does your reaction tend towards denotative meanings or towards the connotative? If you were to write a contract for the sale of horses, you might have to know something about the technical, denotative meanings of the term "horse," no matter what your dominating impression of the animal might be; but if you wanted to ride one, you would be better off having a knowledge of a great many connotative meanings.

What should be included in the denotative definition of "horse"? Such questions often lead writers near to the brink of total frustration, for boundaries are devilishly difficult to establish when one has only logic for fence material; but the anxieties raised are precisely the kind that lawyers have to live with constantly. Only a Supreme Court Justice can afford the luxury of quipping, as one has done concerning the definition of "hard core pornography," that he does not know how to define it, but he knows it when he sees it. Let us take a look at what the most thorough dictionary of the English language felt it should include under the listing "horse."

The Oxford English Dictionary, perhaps the greatest scholarly achievement in English is a work you should grow to know intimately. It took a large team of scholars over 50 years to issue the thirteen huge volumes (first published in 1933), and it now keeps a substantial staff constantly employed, preparing supplements in order to bring the work up to date. A Supplement was needed in 1933 even as the first edition appeared. The second Supplement started to appear in the 1970's, and it comprises three extremely thick volumes. The whole original is available in a two-volume edition, complete with (necessary) magnifying glass. If you do not care to own one, you should become friendly with your library's copy of the work. It is familiarly and reverently referred to as "the *OED*."*

The *OED* expends some 18,000 words in defining "horse," many of which are used in examples portraying the word in context. (18,000 words is the equivalent of a 60-page manuscript.) The number one meaning sounds quite Bitzerian:

> "A solid-hoofed perissodactyl quadruped (*Equus Caballus*), having a flowing mane and tail, whose voice is a neigh. It is well known in the domestic state as a beast of burden and draught, and esp. as used for riding upon."

Even if "horse" (which may come from Teutonic and Latin roots meaning "to run") originally meant only this, no human force could possibly have restrained the word from expanding and contracting. New meanings for a word like "horse" do not replace the old, but rather add to it.

The second major meaning:

> 1.c. "The adult male of the horse kind, as distinguished from a mare or a colt; a stallion or gelding. 'To take the horse': (of the mare) to conceive."

One can imagine how this meaning might have come about. A farmer owned a number of horses. The farmer wished to distinguish between the males, the females, and the children, so he used a word different from "horse" for the latter two categories, using "horse" only for the male. Thus, while all of them continue to be referred to collectively as "horses," any particular animal would more properly be referred to as "horse," "mare," or "colt," depending on its sex and age. Since the new distinction was based on the animal's family structure, it was natural for the word to engender a phrase concerning procreation: "to take the horse."

Meaning 1.c., above, narrows the primary meaning. Meaning 1.d. expands it:

> 1.d. "In *Zoology*. Sometimes extended to all species of the genus *Equus*, or even of the family *Equidae*."

---

* Some sources will refer to it as the *NED*, the initials of its previous title, *The New English Dictionary*.

Meaning 1.e. begins the exploration of sub-species, kinds of horses:

> 1.e. "With qualifications denoting origin, variety, or use, as *Arabian, Barbary, Flemish, wild horse.* Cf. also CART-, DRAY-, SADDLE-, War-Horse, etc.

Once we admit these kinds of variations, we open a floodgate of meanings and metaphors, all of which must be accounted for if the definition is to be complete. The second series of meanings deals with the "representation, figure, or model of a horse." For example:

> "2.b The constellation of Pegasus: . . . Also the equine part of Saggitarius (represented as a centaur)."

We are directed to the entries on "hobby-horse" and "rocking-horse."

Then we proceed to metaphors that stem from uses of the horse, characteristics of the horse, and other animals that have been considered in some way horse-like.

> 3. *Military.* A horse and his rider; hence a cavalry soldier.
>
> 3.c *Horse and foot*: both divisions of an army; hence, whole forces; +advb. with all one's might.
>
> 4. *figurative.* Applied contemptuously or playfully to a man, with reference to various qualities of the quadruped.
>
> 5. Applied to other animals. a. = BLUE-FISH. b. See SEA-HORSE. c. *Horned Horse*, an appellation of the GNU, a species of antelope.

From there the definition moves on to "things resembling the quadruped in shape use, or some characteristic real or fancied," and we find nine more meanings.

> 6. A contrivance on which a man rides, sits astride, or is carried, as on horseback.
>
> 7. A frame or structure on which something is mounted or supported. (Often having legs.)
>
> 8. An instrument, appliance, or device, for some service suggesting or taken to suggest that of a horse.
>
> 9. Six nautical meanings listed here.
>
> 10. a. A lottery ticket hored out by the day.
>   b. A day-rule. *Legal slang.*

11. A mass of rock or earthy matter enclosed within a lode or vein (usually part of the rock through which the lode runs); a fault or obstruction in the course of a vein; hence *to take horse.*

12. (See quot.): "Metallic iron, not finding heat enough in a lead furnace to keep it sufficiently fluid to run out with the slag, congeals in the hearth and forms what smelters term 'sows,' 'bears,' 'horses,' or 'salamanders.' "

13. A translation or other illegitimate aid for students in preparing their work; a "crib."

14. *slang.* Among workmen, work charged for before it is executed.

From #8 on, with the possible exception of #13 (which has recently diminished from "horse" to "pony" and also transformed into "trot"), general knowledge fails us increasingly. We learn there are many "horses" we never knew existed. We have to wait for the Supplements to find "horse" meaning either the piece of equipment used in gymnastics or the slang term for heroin.

All these, however, are only the meanings for the word when it is used by itself. There follows a list of 33 phrases which use the word, each transforming its meaning slightly. Here we find "on horse," "to horse," "gift horse," "high horse," and the like.

Still more: There follows 249 combination words that use "horse," including such relatively uncommon items as "horse-billiards," "horse-names," "horse-nibbled," "horse-mithridate," "horse-twitcher," "horse-ant," "horse-winkle," "horse-cress," "horse-gog," and "horse-purslane."

That completes "horse" as a noun in the main body of the 1933 edition of the Dictionary. The meanings of "horse" used as a verb follow, which include another dozen major individual meanings and many more combinations.

Then we find another 92 separate listings, all of which are "horse"-based, but important enough to merit a listing of their own, words like "horseshoe," "horsewhip," and "horseradish," as well as the lesser known "horse-mackerel," "horse-godmother," and that delightful adverb "horsefully."

The *Supplement* published in 1933 lists yet another 72 meanings and combinations, to which the *Supplement* of 1976 adds another

67. Altogether there are well over 550 listings based on "horse," a number to overwhelm even the most encyclopaedic Bitzer.

As complex as the denotative meanings of "horse" might seem, they still do not begin to succeed in communicating to us the knowledge that Sissy Jupe, the Circus girl, has about horses. She responds to the word differently from Mr. Gradgrind not only because they differ substantially in their sense of what is important in life, but also because of the intrinsic nature of words. What does "horse" connote for a girl who has grown up with a circus?

(a) A particular smell;

(b) A particular sound;

(c) A particular sight or combination of sights (e.g., horse sleeping, horse prancing, horse resisting, horse playing, etc.);

(d) Hard work to be done;

(e) A sense of potential danger;

(f) Familiarity in an otherwise changing set of surroundings, therefore security;

(g) Memories of her father;

(h) Memories of previous experiences with the animals.

Note the connection between "association" and "connotation." Through the repeated associations with a set of experiences and feelings, a word takes on connotations that make the reader or listener recall those associations. A given word, then, should comprise many denotative meanings, which are agreed upon by all and knowable by all, as well as many connotative meanings, which may differ substantially from person to person, depending on previous experience with the word and all that it recalls.

"Horse" is far from the lengthiest entry in the *OED* and far from being the most complex of words, yet its plethora of meanings can be quite overwhelming. We are being foolishly egocentric if we think we know exactly what the word must mean in its every appearance. The more we assume that we are looking at a word (or argument, or concept, or conclusion, or set of facts) in the only sensible way that it can be looked at, the further away we will be from being "the master," and the more easily our opponents, adversaries or detractors will be able to reinterpret those words to their purpose. Thorough knowledge of the denotative meanings of words is essential; we cannot proceed in legal matters without it. Yet to that we must add the knowledge of connotative meanings, else we find ourselves left with a sterile, inhuman knowledge of things.

No man is equipped for modern thinking until he has understood the anecdote of Agassiz and the fish:

A post-graduate student equipped with honours and diplomas went to Agassiz to receive the final and finishing touches. The great man offered him a small fish and told him to describe it.

Post-Graduate-Student: "That's only a sunfish."

Agassiz: "I know that. Write a description of it."

After a few minutes the student returned with the description of the Ichthus Heliodiplodokus, or whatever term is used to conceal the common sunfish from vulgar knowledge, family of Heliichtherinkus, etc., as found in textbooks of the subject.

Agassiz again told the student to describe the fish.

The student produced a four-page essay. Agassiz then told him to look at the fish. At the end of three weeks the fish was in an advanced state of decomposition, but the student knew something about it.[2]

(Erza Pound. *ABC of Reading*)

B. AMBIGUITY AS A PROBLEM IN DEFINITION

The fictitious Thomas Gradgrind was searching for precision in definition, which, he theorized, was the only road to the recognition of reality. In law school you may well come to suspect that there is no such thing as "reality," simply because absolute precision in definition seems impossible to achieve. Law schools consider it their pedogogical responsibility to stretch your thinking powers to the extreme, and they often use the definitional process as an introductory cold shower to wake you up. The following is my own eye-witness account of such a rude awakening.

---

2. Ezra Pound, *ABC of Reading* (London: Faber & Faber, 1963), pp. 17-18.

Two days before my first law classes were to begin, I wandered through the halls, looking at the rooms in which I was to study, reading the notices on the bulletin boards, and trying to get a general sense of what the place was like. One notice on the bulletin board stunned me: It was a list of assignments, one for each of the courses I was to take, which were to be prepared for the first day of class. We had no other warning about this; apparently the faculty wanted to reward those of us who were curious enough to look about us. We were all so chillingly competitive and frighteningly jealous of each other that few of those lucky enough to stumble upon the assignments told anyone else of their discovery.

Two days later I attended my first class, Criminal Law, which was taught by a famous and frightening young professor (the youngest to be tenured in the history of the school), his crew-cut bristling and his eyes shining, seemingly with no light of benevolence. 150 of us sat in the tiered seats, semi-circularly surrounding the professor, who seemed to glare downwards from far above, even though he actually spoke from below us in the amphitheatre. There was no word of welcome, no self-introduction, no exposition of what we were to expect in the course. He scanned the seating chart as if it were a menu and finally decided to devour the victim in seat #79. "Mr. Johnson." Boy number 79, Johnson, rose from his seat with some misgiving, but heartened by the fact that he was one of the lucky ones to have discovered the assignment notices. "Mr. Johnson," the professor repeated, "What was the holding in the Robinson case?" Johnson smiled, even flushed a bit with confidence. "The holding in the Robinson case," he stoutly responded, "was that you cannot convict an individual of the crime of alcoholism, because alcoholism is an illness and beyond the individual's control. The professor clasped his hands, nodded his head, started to pace, and smiled, not at all discretely, all of which seemed to say, "Gotcha." Johnson, all the while, beamed with the light of his new-found success; he would clearly make Law Review and be admired by all as "that fellow who knew everything, even on the first day of class." "Tell me, Mr. Johnson," the professor drawled, taking his time like an animal that knows it has cornered its prey, "What is an 'illness'?" Johnson was shaken. He had expected any sort of legalistic question. He had even done a bit of research on the legal history of alcoholism in Florida and had taken notes. He could quote from them or refer to his new card catalogue in which he had filed the names and citations of the cases he had encountered in his research; but he was not at all prepared for such a simple and disarming question, on a topic any highschooler could handle. "An illness" (here he hesitated for the first time) "is   .   .," and he constructed a definition that anyone could recognize, but that any thinker trained in logic could demolish. "You mean to tell me, Mr. Johnson, that _____ would be an illness?", countered the professor, taking Johnson's definition and subjecting it to a situation which made it ludicrous. "Why no, of course not" (here Johnson sputtered a bit for the first time). "What I meant was   .   .   .," and he repaired the hole that the professor had knocked in the definition. "Aha, I see," said the professor. "Then instead you mean to tell me   .   .   .," and he knocked a different, equally embarrassing hole in another part of the definition. Johnson shifted his weight from one foot to the other and played with his pencil. "Well, actually   .   .   .," and he repaired the second hole. "In that case   .   .   .," said the professor, turning it upside down and punching a new, far more devastating hole. No one looked at Johnson any longer, for we saw in him a Doppelgänger, a ghostly double of ourselves: There, but for the grace of God, or the arrangement of the seating chart, go I.

Johnson never sat down during that first class. For 50 minutes the professor continued to destroy each of his initially proud, then noble, and finally pathetic attempts to define "illness." When we left the room (the bell having mercifully sounded, but too late to save Mr. Johnson), we were convinced that (a) there was no such thing as "illness," because it could not be defined with any hope of consistency; (b) no legal opinion should ever be handed down which used the word, because only logical havoc would follow; and (c) we would all have been reduced to the same pool of sweat from which Johnson emerged at the end, wilted.

The professor could have used any abstract word, perhaps any word at all. "Illness" just happened to be handy.

If we persist in thinking of words as fixed things, we will never gain the perspective to see how others, especially others whose interests are opposed to ours, might see them. Johnson had a good idea of what "illness" was: In fact, he nearly experienced it as he tried to define it. He was unable, however, to convince someone who did not want to be convinced that the phrase or the word had one meaning, or any meaning whatsoever. As a result, the whole class began to realize how much hidden ambiguity plagued even the most straightforward of sentences when exposed to the scrutiny of a well-trained lawyer.

Ambiguity poses a greater danger to thought and communication even than words which are straightforwardly nonsensical. In the case of the latter, the reader knows something has gone amiss; but with the former, the reader gets the impression that one thing has been communicated when the writer has intended quite another. Perhaps most dangerous of all, the ambiguity hides from the writer the fact that the intended thought has not been communicated. When that happens, the contamination may spread to all the acts and thoughts affected by the writing, and a downward spiral will have been initiated that is difficult to arrest.

To diminish the chances for such ambiguity the writer can do the following:

(1) Define important terms *ad hoc*, stating what they mean and marking their boundaries (an extreme solution, but efficient when a central term or two dominates the meaning of the whole piece of writing);

(2) Narrow the logical choices of meaning by making the context in which the word appears as precise as possible;

(3) Use the word in several contexts, which will have the effect of defining and limiting it for the purposes of the present writing (a combination of the first two suggestions).

It sounds like a lot of effort because it is; but without that effort your writing cannot hope to communicate effectively and accurately to others.

That is why an intelligent man cares for his terminology and gives instructions that fit. When his orders are clear and explicit they can be put into effect.   An intelligent man is neither inconsiderate of others nor futile in his commanding.[3]

(Ezra Pound, *Guide to Kulchur*)

C.   THE POWER OF DEFINITION

The act of definition, whether of a word or a concept, is the forging of an agreement where to draw boundaries.   The largest body of people affected by the word generally makes the definitive decision concerning the boundaries.   Although it may appear that we have delegated these responsibilities to lexicographers (the makers of dictionaries), a comparison of any two major dictionaries' pronouncements on any dozen words will demonstrate how little agreement there can be on the fine details that constitute the edges of meanings.   We have, in fact, not created a priesthood of word-makers, but instead have reserved for every private interest group the right to rule its own vocabulary.

The medical profession, for instance, controls all of its own terminology, both in terms of creating new words and assigning new meanings to words in common usage.   A striking example of the latter is one of the medical uses of the word "positive": To most of us the word has a strongly non-negative connotation, but to a doctor who has just performed a biopsy, the word has only negative connotations.

We have empowered our legislative and judicial bodies with the ability to create, limit, and uncreate through its power to redefine the terms used in statutes and holdings.   We might even say, without too much fear of exaggeration, that definition, especially of concepts, constitutes their single most important task.   Note, however, that the Executive branch is not so empowered by us, although it tries time and again to take over that role when it thinks no one is noticing.   For example, one recent administration decided that the best way to prevent a recession was to redefine the word, making it a state of affairs we were unlikely to encounter in the near future.   The government could then proclaim

---

3. Ezra Pound, *Guide to Kulchur*
(New York: New Directions, 1968), p.
17.

with confidence that we were not currently in a recession nor likely to be, as long as the present administration was in charge. The stratagem failed: Journalists quickly pierced the all too thin veil, and the administration let the incident die a quiet death.

The same administration tried to redefine a whole process in much the same way. It discovered that Big Business would save some $2,700,000,000 if the term of depreciation for certain kinds of machinery and equipment was decreased from five years to three. The Executive branch simply announced the change in the boundaries Congress had established, urging Business to rely upon it, only to be frustrated by the quick action of a young lawyer (just five months out of law school). He remembered from his Administrative Law class that such changes in definition cannot be accomplished by executive fiat, but rather require six months of open hearings before administrative boards. The government capitulated immediately, and the statement was withdrawn.

Our system recognizes the enormity of the power to define, and the bodies entrusted with it tend to move slowly and cautiously. In particular, the Law is often the last to change, long after individuals and even society as a whole has become comfortable with a concept. "No-fault divorce," for example, was practiced by the parties concerned, the lawyers, and the judges in a grand collusion (that even necessitated perjury) long before the legislatures of a few states were bold enough to write it into the laws. One conservative state's law had long defined the minimum requirement for "cruel and abusive treatment" (the most common grounds for divorce there) to be actual physical abuse on three different occasions, either the act or the fresh results of the act being witnessed by a third party. Married couples who could no longer abide cohabitation learned that if they could find a friend who was willing to perjure himself or herself by testifying to three fictitious slaps, the court would be willing to wink in sympathy, would not press the issue, and would issue the decree of divorce. Such was the practice for decades, until the legislature decided to make a new law to accord with the reality.

The power of definition, however, is often a private matter, not only for the writer who can through publication choose meanings for words at will (cf. the redefinition of "weak verb" in Chapter II of this text), but also for two or more parties who wish to enter into an agreement with each other. They face only one limitation (although it is a severe one): They may not privately define a word or concept so that it conflicts with a legal precept previously established. Sometimes this clash between private rights and public mandates cannot be easily resolved, and many of the court cases that arise from it make compelling headlines and keep people arguing for many years thereafter. The British case of Regina vs. Dudley and Stevens, 14 Q.B.D. 273 (1884), presented a memorable example.

The defendants and three others were cast adrift in a life boat, their ship having capsized. In a few days their provisions had been consumed, and no help had come into sight. It became clear to them that they would all starve to death unless they found an immediate source of food. They agreed unanimously to draw lots, the loser then to be sacrificed so that his body could provide food for the rest. One passenger was so sacrificed, allowing the others to make it through the next few days, at which time they were saved by a rescue party. They were tried for first-degree murder. Were they guilty? As a society, albeit a small and a temporary one, they had defined their act as a murder of "necessity," considering it parallel to the case of murder in self-defense. Moreover, the court accepted as fact that they would all have died before rescue was possible, had they not killed their companion. Nonetheless, all were convicted of first-degree murder, the decision being upheld by a higher court. Their act fit the British legal system's definition of murder in the first degree, and the court could not allow even this unusual group of private citizens to disregard the law that rules everyone.

When private definitions do not conflict with public law, they become the law until the same individuals choose to alter them. Watch any new society in the action of forming itself, and you will see the debate over the definition process. A dozen fifth-graders go to the park after school to play football. Their first tasks are ones of definition. Who will make up each team? Where will the goal lines be, and where the out-of-bounds lines? How long will they play? How will they know when a given play is ended? (a tag with one hand? two hands? a tackle?) Who will get the ball first?

The same holds true for two parties agreeing to a real estate deal. What will they consider "just compensation"? What will be the time limit for payment? What are the physical limits of the property in question? What will constitute default? None of these answers can be found in dictionaries, nor in statutes, nor in previous court cases, although all of these can help the parties shape their definitive decisions. To avoid future conflict, all parties must agree upon what they intend their relationship to be and that the words they are using do indeed articulate those intentions. It may sound simple enough, but words keep slipping away from you just when you think you have them nailed down securely. A closer look at the difficulties of the definition process will demonstrate to what extent this is true.

D.   A PRACTICAL PROBLEM OF DEFINITION

Problem: A new township wishes to state clearly in its laws that it will be illegal for anyone to leave a car, truck, bus, or other mode of transportation in such a position as to block the access of firefighters to fire hydrants. One town counsellor suggests:

No one may park his car near a fire hydrant.

Several people object. One points out that this would allow one to park a truck there. "Car" is deleted in favor of "Vehicle."

No one may park his vehicle near a fire hydrant.

Another complains of the vagueness of "near." How is anyone to know how near is "near"? In order for a regulation to apply to all people equitably, all people must know as precisely as possible what is expected of them. Vagueness creates opportunities for dictatorial rule and the harrassment of selected individuals. After much debate, "near" is deleted in favor of "within six feet."

No one may park a vehicle within six feet of a fire hydrant.

Yet another person questions the boundaries of the concept "to park." Should it include stopping the car with the driver still at the wheel? If so, how is that to be distinguished from stopping for a red light while parallel to a hydrant? Should "live parking" be allowed, since the car could be moved upon the arrival of a fire engine? Again with much debate, a new configuration is agreed upon.

No one may leave a vehicle unattended within six feet of a fire hydrant.

Most people seem satisfied and are ready to retire for the evening, but one detractor remains. What, he worries, is meant by "within"? From what point on the hydrant is the six feet to be measured? From the point nearest the unattended vehicle? From the point furthest from the vehicle? From the midpoint of the fire hydrant? From the point of the attachment for the nozzle of the fire hose? The decision could make as much a difference as a foot and a half, a substantial percentage of the six feet in question. Furthermore, how much of the vehicle has to intrude upon the six-foot radius for the "vehicle" to be "within" the six-foot radius? A millimeter? A foot? More than half the car? After yet longer debate, everyone wearily accepts the following ungainly, legalistic sounding sentence:

No one may leave a vehicle unattended so that any part of it comes within six feet of the part of a fire hydrant nearest to the vehicle.

Still ambiguities persist. What does "unattended" suggest? Is one "attending" a vehicle by standing next to it, keys in hand? Or by keeping a close watch from a telephone booth at the corner while making a quick call? Or by assigning an employee from one's store the task of watching the vehicle? Must one actually be inside the vehicle to "attend" it? If so, must one be in the driver's seat? Or in possession of the keys and a valid driver's license?

Will the town need yet another law to prevent people from leaving objects other than vehicles (e.g., garbage cans) near enough to fire hydrants to obstruct easy access to them? What problems might arise by attempting to incorporate such restrictions into the law about vehicles? The questions could continue.

One might have considered the concept "Don't block access to fire hydrants" an easy one to articulate. We all know what we mean by it, and the benefit to society seems unambiguous. No conflicts with any other human rights spring to mind. ("It's a free country, so I'll park wherever I like" hardly represents a reasonable point of view.) Why, then, has this "clear" concept generated so many questions and difficulties? Could it be that the very simplicity of the appearance of the task masked the possible pit-falls so that the first attempts at formulation merely served as reminders of, not articulations of, the agreed upon idea? "No one may park his car near a fire hydrant" refers to the prohibition in question but does not define the boundaries.

Although it seemed a simple enough task, the fire hydrant problem actually presents too complex a definition task at this stage of our progress. That one problem comprises the sub-problems of defining several concrete objects and several abstract entities and then relating them all to each other. To make matters more clear, we should first look at the process of defining a concrete object; then we can move on to abstract entities; and by then we should be better prepared to attempt complexes of concepts.

Any definition whatever must strive towards a double goal:

(A) To include everything that is necessary to the existence of that which is being defined; and

(B) To exclude anything that is unnecessary.

This double task requires the definer to consider all possible uses of the term(s) or concept(s), not just those which are associated with the situation which originally triggered the need for the definition (cf. the fire hydrant problem above). We must not expect to find an objective answer at the end of our labors, but rather we must be prepared to accept a compromise, a definition that most of us can "live with" for all practical purposes.

EXERCISE

A city includes the following in its traffic regulations:

A vehicle may legally proceed through a yellow light as long as the vehicle is within the intersection by the time the light turns red.

(1) Interpret this regulation in as much detail as you can. What are the ambiguities? What are the possible injustices or nonsensical situations that could develop from it?

(2) If this regulation is adopted by the hypothetical town of this chapter, will there be any conflicts between their fire hydrant law and their yellow light law? Explain.

E. THE DEFINITION OF A CONCRETE OBJECT

"Bicycle." If our definition cannot be applied with complete accuracy to all bicycles, we have failed. If it can be applied to something that does not qualify as a bicycle, we again have failed. Who is to say what is or is not a "bicycle"? We are.

We must not merely describe, we must define. Though many a bicycle may have a red ribbon or blue racing stripes, we cannot include those colorful items in our definition unless we wish to make them required of all bicycles.

We can proceed by formulating essential questions and then answering them. Any questions that lead us into the consideration of the basic requirements for "bicycle" will do, for it does not matter where we start, as long as we have covered everything by the time we finish. We can test "completeness" by the double goal articulated above, asking whether the final product includes everything necessary and excludes all that is unnecessary.

For concrete objects, the following three questions will always elicit valuable responses:

What does it do?

What are its essential component parts?

How does it function?

We can test each individual answer by two methods:

    (1) By rephrasing the answer into a negative conditional clause and asking if we still have a "bicycle"—

        Question: What does it do?

        Answer: It does "X."

        Test: If it does not do "X," can it still be a bicycle?

    (2) By asking if all bicycles conform to the answer—

        Question: What does it do?

        Answer: It does "X."

        Test: Do all bicycles do "X"?

What does a bicycle do? It transports. Since a bicycle is a bicycle even when it is not in the very action of transporting, we should speak of its potential for transporting: "A bicycle is a means of transportation." It is capable of doing other things, like propping open a door or serving as a model for an art class, but those functions are not essential to its existence as a bicycle, nor do they distinguish "bicycle" from other weighty objects.

When we apply the two tests suggested above, we can see definitional problems arising already.

Question: What does a bicycle do?

Answer: It is a means of transportation.

Test: If it is not a means of transportation, can it still be a bicycle?

Test: Are all bicycles means of transportation?

The test questions force us to consider the importance of the life span of a "bicycle." If a bicycle has been used for ten years and has deteriorated so much that it can no longer be used as a means of transportation (at least in its current condition), is it still a "bicycle"? Our answer to this question will in turn depend on our reason for defining the term in the first place. If we are members of the Department of Transportation trying to formulate legislation that will tax all vehicles, then we might be willing to exclude the old machine from the category of "bicycle," since in its present state it cannot function as a vehicle and therefore is of no concern to us. We would want to know only about machines that help people get around. If, on the other hand, we are a committee from the Department of Defense trying to account for all potentially available vehicles in case of a war, then the old machine, if repairable, might well be of interest to us, and we would continue to categorize it as a "bicycle."

What are its component parts? We must speak of wheels, for no one would recognize a wheel-less object as a bicycle; but how many wheels it might or must have presents another problem altogether. "Bi-cycle" would seem to indicate two wheels, but words have often strayed far from their etymological origins. If it has three wheels, we tend to call it a "tricycle," which we usually associate with children only. What, then, should we call the three-wheeled vehicles ridden by the elderly nowadays, "tricycles" or "bicycles" (or perhaps even something completely different)? If a two-wheeled cycle has two extra "training wheels" attached, is it no longer a "bicycle"? If so, does that qualify it or disqualify it as a "bicycle"? What would the hypothetical Departments of Transportation and Defense say about it? Should a bicycle owner be able to avoid paying a tax on a "bicycle" by attaching two training wheels to it just before the tax collector arrives at the door? If the government needed a bicycle for transportation in war time, should it not be allowed to take two training wheels off and requisition the vehicle? We would need to come to agreements on these and all other questions about the number of wheels. Although no one answer or decision might completely please us, we find ourselves forced to settle with one, and we must remain consistent to that decision once we have made it.

If you are starting to suspect that most of the details we might consider would involve the same kinds of hidden problems and require the same kinds of compromises and subjective decisions, then you are on the right track. If we were to investigate every detail in full here, this would become a book about bicycles, perhaps a good-sized one, at that. There is space here only to raise some of the questions, without an attempt to answer them.

—Need we include anything about a seat in our definition?

Can we have a bicycle without a seat?

Do all bicycles have seats?

—Should we refer to handlebars?

Have you ever seen a bicycle without handlebars?

Could you imagine a bicycle without handlebars, and does that matter?

Why would we want to include handlebars?

If a Committee on Public Safety decreed, "All bicycles must have handlebars," would they be including or excluding handlebars from their definition of "bicycle"?

—Must we mention chains and gears?

Can we mention chains and gears?

—Concerning the function of a bicycle, must we specifically exclude motors? Must a "bicycle" be a person-powered vehicle?

Should a motored vehicle that otherwise conforms to our definition of "bicycle" be considered a bicycle if it is used with the motor off?

—Need it be solo operated?

Is a tandem a "bicycle," or is it distinguishable as something different, a "bicycle-built-for-two"?

We must exclude from our definition many items that would appear most prominently were we writing a description instead: horns, bells, baskets, lights, reflectors, etc. Even if some of these could pass our second test (e.g., perhaps today all bicycles have reflectors), they still would fail our first test: We would agree, probably, that a bicycle which has had its reflectors ripped off is still a bicycle. By contrast, a bicycle without a wheel we might well not consider a "bicycle" until the wheel had been replaced. These distinctions are neither easy to make nor easy to understand, but they are crucial to the kind of thinking that a lawyer must do.

EXERCISE

Define one of the following as thoroughly as possible. Be sure your definition achieves the double goal outlined above on page 137.

  (a) Book

  (b) Razor

  (c) Pen

  (d) Chair

F. THE DEFINITION OF AN ABSTRACT ENTITY

------

1. THE CONCEPT OF "TEAM"

The questions raised about the definition of "bicycle" should have demonstrated that we cannot clearly separate the concrete from the abstract. The moment we ask a question about the object "bicycle," we are treating it as an abstract as well as tangible entity. When we push further on, we find ourselves wondering about the concept of "bicycleness." The separate categories, therefore, do not represent thought distinction, but only allow for a progression of complexity as we consider the nature of definition.

Now we will look at an abstract entity, in this case something rather mundane set in a conceptual frame, "football team." In order to define this two-word combination, we must define each word by itself and then consider anything else that arises from the act of combining the two words into one phrase.

What is a "team"? This time let us use a different double test, equally as effective as the one used previously, but perhaps yet easier to apply when dealing with abstractions. Let "X" stand for our final definition, so that we can state "Team = X." Then we ask the following conjunctive questions:

(1) Are all teams "X"?

(2) Are all "X" 's teams?

If the answer is "yes" in both cases, we have a viable definition. Again, it matters not where we start, as long as we have a complete definition by the time we finish. Let us start, then, simply.

A team is a group of people.

This would produce one "yes" and one "no" if subjected to our two-fold test. All teams are indeed groups of people, but not all groups of people are teams. We are therefore looking for a subset of the large set "groups of people." What difference is there between a random group of people and a "team"?

A team is a group of people who share the same specific goal.

Again we can answer "yes" to question #1, but "no" to question #2. A group of people gathered at a street corner waiting for the light to change all share the same goal or interest, but we would not refer to them as a "team"; nor would we use the term to refer to all scientists in the country who are working on a cure for cancer. Something still is missing.

Beyond the sense of "group" we find a sense of "many individuals" in the concept of "team." If we compare all the teams we can think of to see what characteristics they have in common, we would discover that although the group as a whole has a single goal, each individual has a separate and distinct task to perform. To make a "group" into a "team," these specific tasks must be coordinated so that they fit together to produce the single, overriding effort towards the common goal. Therefore,

A team is a group of people, each of whom has an individual task that is coordinated with the others to strive towards a common goal.

Thus, if a Federal Agency controlled all cancer research in the country, making special assignments to coordinate all the individual efforts and to avoid duplication of effort, then we could justifiably refer to all cancer researchers as a "team." (This explains why politicians delight in referring to their thousands of campaign workers as a "team." The same holds true for business executives. The term, so used, is likely to be metaphoric, not explicit.)

If we apply our double test to our present definition, we can answer "yes" to both questions.

The same definition could have been reached by asking the questions we asked about "bicycle," although the answers might not have suggested themselves as readily.

What does a team do?

It strives towards a goal.

What are its essential component parts?

It is made up of people, each of whom has an individual task.

How does it function?

All the individual tasks are coordinated so that the common goal can be reached.

2. THE CONCEPT OF "FOOTBALL"

Now we turn to "football," the game. We can distinguish football teams from all other teams only by distinguishing football from all other activities.

Many of the first things that come to mind about "football," strangely enough, have no part in a definition of the game (which, arbitrarily, we shall limit to the American brand): referees in striped shirts, large people in helmets, colored jerseys and bulky padding, bold white lines drawn on a green field—all these are descriptive of organized football, but not part of a definition of the generic term "football," which must include everything from the most informal pick-up game on a sandlot to the Super Bowl in a multi-million dollar stadium. Those dozen fifth-graders we have encountered before can play football without the white lines, the uniforms, and the referees.

What do all football games have in common? If we apply our previously useful categories ("What does it do?"—"What are its essential component parts?"—"How does it function?"), we uncover the following corresponding categories, or something like them: an objective of play; necessary equipment or personnel; and the limitations of play. These categories are not the only ones we might decide to try, but they do provide a helpful starting point.* Let us consider them in reverse order, beginning with the limitations of play.

Playing "football" directly implies restricting all players to the specific set of limitations associated with that game. The fifth-graders mentioned on p. 88 above would have understood this, judging from their actions.

—Limitation of team identity:

Who will be on which team (there being precisely two teams)?

—Limitation of space (the goal lines and the out-of-bounds):

Lines will be drawn, whether imaginary or actual. The fifth-graders might mark only the four corners of the field ("my math book, Ricky's sweater, the big tree, and the water fountain.") As we will see shortly, limitation of space is absolutely essential to the concept of "football." Without it, people would just be playing catch or practicing their football skills, but not be involved in a "football game."

* These three questions will not always be equally helpful. Try them, for example, on the concept "justice."

—Limitation of duration:

They will agree to play either until dark or until Mom calls for dinner or until Joey has to go to his dentist appointment (Joey owns the ball) or until one team scores five times. Without this kind of limitation, as any fifth-grader will be quick to tell you, it is not a "real" game.

—Limitation on possession of the ball:

Here we would have to explain the concept of "offense" and "defense," and that the game is divided into series of discrete "plays" that begin when the ball is lifted from the ground and end by some agreed upon display of defensive skill (by a tag or a tackle or any other means agreed upon). Note that the specific means must not appear in the definition, for that would limit football to only those few. We do need to articulate, however, that some means must exist and be agreed upon.

We would also have to include that (but not how) the possession of the ball changes from one team to another according to the completion of some tasks (scoring) or the failure at some others (not making enough progress in a given number of plays).

All of these limitations are essential to our definition because without any one of them we stray from what the public at large understands by the term "football game." * It is important to understand the principles by which we include some details and exclude others. It depends upon the universality of the particular occurrence. We must mention something about the general ways the ball is advanced down the field, because these are used in all football games, and this particular combination of techniques is found in no other sport. On the other hand, we must not name positions (Quarterback, Wide Receiver, Weak Safety, etc.) in a definition because these terms vary from team to team, depending on the formality of the organization, and upon the passage of time. The term "Nose Guard" in 1960 might have referred to a part of the helmet; now it refers to a centrally located defensive lineman on those teams that use a three-man defensive line.

* We can also debate whether "football," as used in "football team," implies the concept "football game"; but to avoid excess complications, we will let that pass.

No mention of "Nose Guard," therefore, may invade our definition. We would not want to have to abandon the term "football" because some inventive coach thinks up a new defensive alignment which makes Nose Guard a thing of the past.

The question of equipment narrows down to a consideration of the necessity of the ball itself, and no more. All the padding, goal posts, kicking tees, and special cleats can be dispensed with without affecting the concept of "football game." The inclusion of any of them would exclude many legitimate forms of football from our definition. We can, however, argue at some length about the necessity of the specially shaped ball that is so closely associated with American football. All else being equal, can one play a "football game" with something other than a football? Are the people who play by football rules and customs but use a frisbee instead of the traditional ball (1) playing "football" with a frisbee, or (2) playing another sport altogether, called "frisbee-football"?

When we come to consider "the objective of play," we arrive at the heart of the defining process, for here we must discover both what the purpose of a football game is (existence) and what distinguishes it from other sports or activities (uniqueness). These lines of definition are far from easy to draw, even in a case such as this, where only intellectual rigor is at stake. When legislators drawing up a law or individuals drawing up an agreement encounter the problem, they are faced with both the requirements of intellectual rigor and potentially substantial, tangible results that could affect the lives of many.

Unfortunately, there exists no simple list of questions that will cover all the considerations of the "objective" of an abstract entity. Fortunately, on the other hand, all those considerations seem to interlock, so that investigating any one will eventually lead round to all the others. It does not matter which leg of a table you make first, as long as when you are finished the thing stands firmly on the ground. We can start, therefore, at the most simplistic response and work from there.

There seem to be two major schools of thought on the subject. Many an officionado will tell you the objective in a football game is "to win"; others will tell you it is "how you play the game" that counts. They sound diametrically opposed, but on closer inspection they are not. Push them both with the question "How?". The first group will talk of scoring points and preventing your opponents from doing the same. The second group will talk of spirited efforts and carrying out assignments and steadfastness. Both groups, it turns out, deal with the process of the game, and both suggest that doing the process well is the major objective.

We still have not articulated what that process is, how the different details of it come together to form a whole, and how that whole is distinguishable from other games.

Football is an adversary process, a variant of the "sum-zero" game, wherein whatever one team possesses must necessarily be an equivalent loss to the other team. To "win" the game is to end up with a greater manifestation of superiority than the others (calculated in this case in "points"). Points in football do not refer to quality level of the actual performance (as, for instance, in figure skating) or quantity of performance (as, for instance, in golf). Points in football reflect the accomplishment of certain tasks which, in turn, reflect skill and control. The scoring system in organized football may appear somewhat arbitrary. A team receives six points for a "touchdown," that is, for its having maintained possession and control of the ball in transporting it past the opponent's goal line. Three points are awarded for a "field goal," that is, the kicking of the ball from the ground through a topless rectangle described by the goal-posts and their crossbar. Two points result from a "safety," which is the tackling of an opponent ball carrier behind his own goal line. One or two points (depending on the league which controls the game) may be awarded as "extra points," the opportunity for which comes only after a team has scored a touchdown; the clock is stopped, and the scoring team is given one chance to score again, this time from the three-yard line. How do all these scoring feats relate to one another? How can one define what it is to score in football? It seems essential to understand this, since the objective of the game has something to do with playing well enough to score more points than the opponent.

In order to score many points, a team must be able to move the ball downfield continually. All forms of football put some limit on a team's "possession" of the ball, allowing a certain number of "plays" or attempts in which some kind of competence must be demonstrated to allow the team to continue its ownership. In college and professional play in the United States, for instance, a team must move the ball ten yards closer to the opponent's goal in four plays in order to retain possession. Since no other sport has this requirement, we must be getting closer to understanding football's uniqueness.

The concept of individual plays also distinguishes this sport from many others. Unlike soccer, rugby, lacrosse, basketball, and hockey, football is not a sport of continuous action. When a play has ended (which happens when the defensive team manifests its momentary superiority over the offense by some agreed form of contact with the ball carrier or some form of disruption of the play), a "line of scrimmage" is established that lasts until the next play is over. That line of scrimmage is the imaginary line parallel to the goal lines which includes the point where the ball rests. Between plays each team must stay on its own side of the line of scrimmage. It is from this line that the measurements are made that determine how far the offensive team has progressed. Again we have come upon something unique to football: The line of scrimmage marks the starting point for each play. As it turns out, this imaginary line plays a central role in the overall definition of the objective of a football game.

Putting some of these details together, a concept starts to emerge. Play begins at a line of scrimmage; a team continues to possess the ball as long as its plays are successful enough to gain substantial portions of ground within a given number of plays; and between the plays teams are not allowed on the opponent's side of the line of scrimmage. What, then, has this to do with the scoring of points? Not until we can connect the process of play with the rewards of doing that process effectively can we understand what "winning" or "playing well" means.

Picture a football field before and after a play in which the offensive team gains fifteen yards. Arbitrarily choosing the thirty yard line as the initial line of scrimmage, the field possession would look like this before the play:

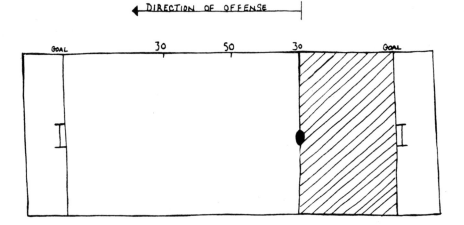

The shaded portion represents the portion of the field that the offensive team "owns," the unshaded area between the line of scrimmage and their goal line. Either team will be penalized for encroaching on the other's "territory" before the ball is put into play. After the play, in which the offensive team gains fifteen yards, the field looks like this:

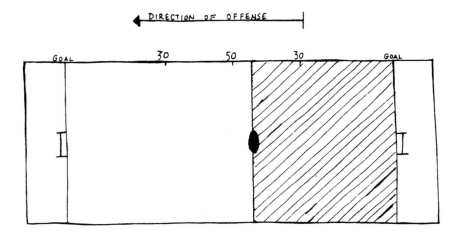

In this "sum-zero" process, the offense now owns fifteen yards more than it did, as a result of the defensive team's having lost fifteen of its yards. (Adding the plus fifteen to the minus fifteen, the "sum" is "zero.")

On the next play, let us hypothesize, the offense hurls a dramatic 55-yard pass and scores a touchdown. At the end of that play the field of possession would look like this:

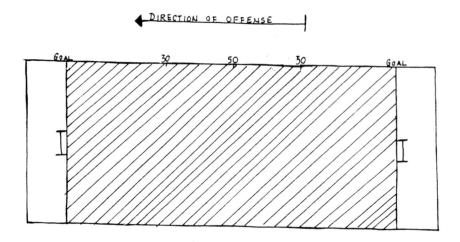

It seems we have found the principle behind the process. Football turns out to be a game of real estate. When one team owns all of the real estate (as defined by the goal lines and the placement of the line of scrimmage), then it is awarded six points, called a "touchdown."

The other manners of scoring conform to this theory in one way or another. A field goal (three points) is awarded when the offensive team owns so much real estate that it is close enough to the opponent's goal to kick the ball with accuracy through the posts. A safety (two points) is awarded to the defensive team when it has managed to capture all of the offense's real estate (the line of scrimmage being pushed behind the offensive goal line, leaving 100% of the field to the defense). The extra point is indeed "extra" to the game, it being executed apart from the time allotted to the game and the three yards needed to score it being arbitrary and unconnected to any actual play by the offense. (The probable purpose of the extra point was to make it possible for one touchdown to be worth more than two field goals.)

The central objective of a football game, then, may be seen as the control of real estate, extreme control producing a variety of points scored. Points, conversely, are the manifestations of the extent of control achieved. The game could have been measured by the straightforward calculation of territory captured, but compelling considerations of drama, ease of calculation, and player motivation must have convinced the creators that the point system was more attractive than cumulative yard totals. (Note, however, that careful statistics are kept on who has gained how much yardage, and even an inept team will be proud if it produces the individual league leader in yardage at the end of the season).

When we turn later to the consideration of quasi-legal problems, we will see how important it is to penetrate through the details of a situation to its underlying principles, as we have managed to do for "football." The importance extends far beyond a sense of neatness and order in identifying things accurately; it reaches all the way to the ability to use the concept in future situations in a consistent fashion. If we do not understand why certain details exist, then we cannot tell if we are doing harm to the whole concept by changing, removing, or adding details. The following exercise will give you an opportunity to experiment with this notion.

EXERCISE

When does a change in detail change the concept of the whole? Hypothetical: Pro Football fans, the polls reveal, are frustrated by tie games, and 74% say they would prefer any tie-breaking system whatever to allowing games to remain deadlocked at the end. The television networks, however, suddenly decide not to broadcast any more than the four quarters of regulation play for games next season because of the concomitant scheduling problems and because others of their clients who are affected by the overtime games are threatening court action if overtime matches are encouraged. Due to the financial impact of full television coverage, the professional football league decides against using overtime periods in any but championship games. After much consultation and many meetings, two proposals are made, one of which must be chosen to go into effect for next season:

(A) If the teams are tied at the end of regulation time, the game will be awarded to the team which has controlled the ball for the longer period of time (the time being figured cumulatively throughout the game), as long as there is at least a five-minute difference in cumulative times. If the difference is less than five minutes, the game is declared a tie.

(B) If the teams are tied at the end of regulation time, the game will be awarded to the team which has gained more yardage (the yardage being figured cumulatively through-out the game), as long as there is at least a 75-yard difference in cumulative yardage. If the difference is less than 75 yards, the game is declared a tie.

Task: Make a thorough argument for adapting the second pro-posal, based on the above discussion of the nature of football. Suggest alterations for the proposal for the better if you wish, but substantiate all proposed changes with careful argument.

———◆———

Practice in definitional skills will enhance your powers of dis-covering the underlying nature of things, of uncovering the con-cept beneath the word. The seeming paradox of the emphasis on individual task and the emphasis on group achievement that con-stitutes the concept of "team" explains in part why being a team member is so psychologically attractive, why business executives and political candidates like to encourage their workers to think of themselves as forming one large "team." Understanding the con-cept that underlies "football" might help clarify why some people react so intensely towards the sport, some becoming almost irra-tionally involved with the progress of a game, others being com-pletely antagonistic even to the mention of the word.

The definition process helps you to know how to step back from the details of a situation in order to see its organizing principles. By it you can also create an awareness in yourself of your own responses. As you proceed, the emotions involved fade away, and the rational processes take over. From understanding comes control, the power to articulate, the power to communicate, and the power to convince. (Once this is accomplished, it then becomes important to remember and reconsider the emotional response, lest all ethical considerations disappear and you become solely a producer of logic.)

For the practice of Law, the importance of understanding and being able to perform the defining process cannot be exaggerated. Good lawyers understand that words not only can mean, but they can do, as well; words not only articulate, they create. When lawyers choose words to make a contract between their clients, they are not merely recognizing a previously existing relationship, they are creating a new one. Only a keen sense of what words are doing, what they could do, and what they could be made to do (by someone "on the other side") will prevent the contract from becoming a shambles of good intentions, destroyed by inept execution.

Definition takes time, careful consideration, and careful reconsideration. The more common the concept sometimes the more difficult it is to capture exactly what is to be understood by it. You must constantly reconsider the following questions as you proceed:

—Is this detail common to all X's?

—Is this detail necessary in order for it to be an X?

—Does this detail help distinguish X from all non-X's?

Definition must include everything necessary to the thing defined and exclude everything unnecessary. When all is done, the thing must be recognizable from the definition, and nothing that is other than the thing must fit the definition.

EXERCISE

Define one of the following:

(A) Television show

(B) Dinner table

(C) Final examination

(D) Legal rights

To maximize this experience, then exchange definitions with a classmate and rework the two into one agreed upon definition. This process could be continued until the whole class was able to agree upon a single definition.

Chapter V

THE KINDS OF WRITING LAWYERS DO

Classical Rhetoric divided its subject matter into five modes of discourse: Narration, Description, Exposition, Argumentation, and Persuasion. A Narration tells what happened; Description communicates the response the writer had to what happened; Exposition sets forth the writer's thoughts; Argumentation sets forth thought for the purpose of proving it true; and Persuasion sets forth thought, whether true or not, for the purpose of convincing the reader to agree. Although these five modes overlap a great deal, each calls for a different set of writing strategies. A lawyer must control all five and know when to call on each. Having a good sense of the distinctions between these modes can often aid in keeping a writing task clearly defined. Aimless wandering from one to another normally confuses the issues being discussed.

In the last two chapters we concentrated on Definition, an expository process that accounts for a large portion of a lawyer's writing tasks. It involves an act of creation, setting boundaries around a thought so that we can perceive its shape and extent and thereby use it without confusing it for something else. Many of the later chapters will concentrate on Argumentation and Persuasion, the processes by which a writer convinces others to accept these newly defined entities. In this chapter we look at the four main writing tasks of a lawyer, relating them to the different Modes of Discourse, thereby giving you some sense of how your writing skills will be used in the profession.

Most of the formal writing produced by a lawyer falls into one of the following four categories: agreements, briefs, memos, and letters.

A. AGREEMENTS

1. PRECISION AND ANTI-PRECISION

Written agreements, in essence, are privately made law. Two or more parties agree in writing to interact in a certain way, thereby creating rights and responsibilities where previously there may have been none. As long as that agreement does not conflict with another previous agreement, counteract some policy of public law, or fall short of the requirements our courts have established over time, it will effectively bind the parties who have signed it. An agreement can define status or ownership, establish duties and responsibilities, demand action or restraint from action, recognize the past, define the present, or prepare for the future. It calls for extreme accuracy in expository writing, both in terms of precision and anti-precision.

The need for precision might seem obvious to you at this point (having recently considered such imprecise terms as "illness," "bicycle," and "within"), but at the same time you should be starting to understand how extraordinarily difficult exact precision is to attain. A lawyer wishes to leave as little as possible open to question in a written agreement. If a court is called in at some point to interpret some ambiguity, it will concentrate on the text that was agreed to and will not often go in search of missing words or provisions that the parties had forgotten or assumed or inferred. Courts prefer not to get involved with the treacherously uncertain business of the intentions behind non-happenings. (It is difficult enough to discern the intentions behind something that actually has happened.) A lawyer writing an agreement, therefore, must include everything that is necessary to protect the client's interests, leaving nothing for common sense to fill in later. This consideration alone causes legal agreements to extend to intimidating lengths and include such a plethora of detail.

Do not, however, confuse precision with thoroughness. The former produces accuracy, the latter completeness. The lawyer's main difficulty in terms of precision, lies in getting enough distance from the writing to be able to read it with the eyes of one who is either impartial or hostile to the perspective of the writer.

It takes both time and experience to develop this ability, but without it you can never hope to practice law with confidence.

The need for anti-precision (the intentional avoiding of precision) may not be as apparent as the need for precision. The positive use of this term should not be taken to suggest that lawyers must learn to write confusing prose that will trick the other party into reading the agreement one way when it "actually" reads another. Indeed, courts have often invalidated whole contracts on the basis of such ambiguities. Instead, the term "anti-precision" refers to the kind of writing necessitated by our inability to predict accurately what will happen in the future. Many times parties make agreements that function flawlessly under the conditions existing at the time of the writing, but backfire when some unforeseen turn of events confuses the issue. Lawyers need to develop a sense for the different kinds of permanence that result from different kinds of writing, as well as a knowledge of the practical probabilities associated with different kinds of contractual relations. In those cases where future incidents beyond anyone's control can turn an advantageous agreement into a legal straightjacket, the lawyer is well advised to use language that is open-ended ("anti-precise"), taking care that the agreement not become so vague as to be unenforceable. It takes a delicate and well-trained hand to draw such fine lines of distinction. Essentially, the lawyer must state the underlying principles or intentions of the agreement clearly, while allowing a certain amount of leeway for complicating fact situations that might occur.

For example: The city of Newfolk, which has always been run by the Mayor and a few appointed advisors, has grown so large that the inhabitants feel the need for an elected City Council, directly representative of the population, to balance the all too centralized power of the Mayor. The city is neatly divided by the two main streets into four districts, North, South, East, and West, each of which have a population of about 4,000. How should the membership of the Council be determined? How many members should there be, and how should they be apportioned to the districts?

In this situation, absolute precision (for instance, the assigning of 4 seats to each district), might cause a great many problems. At present each district would have one seat for every 1,000 people, a neat enough solution; but in the future several things could happen to destroy this comfortable symmetry:

(1) What if the population shifted in the next ten years so that East Newfolk gained 1,200 people that used to live in West Newfolk? The new center of population would still be represented by four council members, one now for every 1,300 people, while the part of town being deserted, also represented by four members, would control one seat for every 700 people.

(2) What would happen if, instead, the population of each district doubled in the next ten years? Will the precise language that designates four seats to each district now result in diminished representation for everybody? Could you convince a Newfolk court that the "four seats per district" language really had intended that there be one representative for every 1,000 people? If you could, would the resulting Council of 32 members be able to function in the same ways that the previous Council of 16 had? What if the population doubled again? And again? And again?

(3) Imagine that some natural disaster (flood, tornado, or conflagration) devastates South Newfolk so completely that no one is willing to rebuild there, and it becomes totally uninhabited. Speculation Realty, Inc., buys up all of South Newfolk at bargain rates. How much control of the City Council would Speculation have? How much should they have?

Anti-precise language could help the city of Newfolk avoid some of these problems. The written document (essentially an agreement between all the inhabitants) should concentrate on defining the concept of representation. It should also establish standards for the dispersal of seats and methods for changing the Council's size and shape as the size and shape of the city's population changes; but the anti-precise language used in the definition would give future generations a standard for dealing with problems not foreseen by the precise standards and methods articulated.

You may think this a rather simple-minded example, but had the founding fathers of representative government in England understood these problems when they drafted the Magna Carta (A.D. 1215), they would have altered significantly the course of political history. Magna Carta, which established a Parliament to help curb the power of the monarch, assigned two seats to each of the most populous areas of the country, clearly identifying those areas. Nothing could have been more precise.

One of the population centers at that time was Old Sarum, a hilltop in Wiltshire that supported a castle, a cathedral, and a substantial number of people. Soon after 1215 the people of Old Sarum decided they would be much better off if they moved three miles away, to be able to take advantage of the river that flowed by there. By 1255 the castle and the houses were abandoned, and the cathedral had been moved, stone by stone, the distance of three miles to found the new town of Salisbury. (The cathedral still stands and is well worth a visit, as are the ruins of Old Sarum.) Magna Carta, however, had made no provision for such changes, and the abandoned hill continued to send two members to Parliament, while the populous town of Salisbury went unrepresented. (Districts like Old Sarum became known as "Rotten Boroughs" or "Pocket Boroughs," for whoever owned them effectively had two seats in Parliament "in his pocket.") This remarkable state of affairs continued until the Reform Bill of 1832, a testimony to the negative potentialities of precision.

Another example of precision backfiring: In the Nineteenth Century there was a woman in Boston who owned two houses, across the street from each other, near the top of Mt. Vernon Street on Beacon Hill. Because the house she lived in was three stories tall, and the other was only one story, she had a clear view of Boston Commons, where (as the Law still provides) she had the right to graze her cow. It comforted her a great deal to sit in her bay window and be able to check on her cow's well-being during Tea. When her son came of age, she wished to deed to him the property across the street, but she feared he might add to the height of the house, thereby blocking her view. To ensure that this would not happen, she had her lawyers put a clause in the deed that forbade the son (or anyone to whom he sold or to whom they sold, *in perpetuum*) to build higher than one story on that property. (This is known as a contingency that "runs with the land.") The precision of the language succeeded, and the lady and her cow ended their days in peace. The succession of people who have owned that small house on the other side of Mt. Vernon Street have never enjoyed peace, however, for no matter how hard the best law firms of Boston have tried for more than a century, no one has been able to figure out a way around the restriction. If you drive up Mt. Vernon Street today you can still see on your right a continuum of three-story town-houses interrupted only once by a modest looking one-story building.

EXERCISE

Hypothetical:

In 1950, Improvident Realty, Inc., signed a 99-year agreement with We-Go-Along Trailers, Inc., for the rental of a garage-warehouse. Included was a "cost of living" provision:

> The rent shall be $10,000 per annum for the first decade, changing to $20,000 per annum in 1960, likewise to $30,000 in 1970, $40,000 in 1980, and so forth. In addition, for each year of a decade the rent will be increased a percentage of $10,000 equivalent to the Federal Government's official "Cost of Living Index" percentage, should that have increased in that year.

The cost of living increased at 4% per year* from 1950 to 1960, resulting in the following rents being paid by We-Go-Along:

1950	$10,000	1954	11,600	1958	13,200
1951	10,400	1955	12,000	1959	13,600
1952	10,800	1956	12,400	1960	20,000
1953	11,200	1957	12,800		

Improvident had not envisioned the double-digit inflation of the 1980's. At the beginning of that decade analysts predicted the following trends:

1980–1983 — an average of 16% inflation each year

1984–1986 — an average of 20% inflation each year

1987–1988 — an average of 16% inflation each year

Based on these figures, the rent for the 1980's would be the following:

1980	$40,000	1984	46,400	1988	54,000
1981	41,600	1985	48,400	1989	55,600
1982	43,200	1986	50,400		
1983	44,800	1987	52,400		

---

* A hypothetical figure, used here for convenience.

In 1990, as the agreement explicitly states, the rent must be $50,000, which, if the analysts' predictions are accurate, would result in a decrease of $5,600 from the 1989 rent. The agreement therefore would become self-contradictory:

(1) On the one hand it provides for increases to offset inflation;

(2) On the other hand it lists precise rates every ten years which, in times of bad inflation, would counteract the provisions for raising the rent to account for inflation.

The parties take the agreement to a court. The judge invalidates the entire agreement on the grounds of ambiguity. Both parties wish to continue their business relationship on a reasonable basis.

Task: You are hired by Improvident to draw up a new 99-year agreement. Draft a clause that will settle the problem of rent for the next century, remembering that inflation is totally unpredictable over such a period of time.

2. "REDUCING" AN AGREEMENT TO WRITING

Some small business owners still prefer to work with oral agreements instead of trying to pin down every detail in writing.

If I give you my hand on it, I will fulfill the spirit of the contract to its fullest. If we write it down, I will do only what the words say I must do.

(George Liberman, purveyor of barber supplies)

This attitude illustrates an interesting phenomenon generated by the act of "reducing" an agreement to writing. It would seem that by formalizing the agreement in a written document the parties would be able to expand upon the central intentions, enumerating all the necessary details, making everything clear and complete. In many cases, however, the writing will limit the original intentions to only the specifics actually articulated, thereby excluding anything unmentioned, even if it "obviously" accords with the spirit of the transaction.

Most businesses today cannot afford to depend on oral agreements because transactions have become so complex. Since our laws concerning agreements have favored the written form, people who might have to depend on courts for protection and satisfaction know they will be far better off if they "have it in writing." Our attempt here to understand the difference between a written and an oral agreement is not intended, therefore, to encourage greater dependence on the oral, but rather to demonstrate some of the problems that naturally arise from the nature of "reducing" thought to written words. We shall consider two metaphors which try to illustrate the oral/written distinction. The first metaphor is overly simple, but direct; the second is rather subtle, but more revealing.

The simple metaphor: A group of friends get together to plan a gourmet meal, each course of which is to be prepared by a different person. Joe has not done much cooking, but he is such a convivial dinner companion that he is included in the group. To be on the safe side, the group assigns Joe the salad course. Which of the following is wisest? (1) Send Joe to the store to buy ingredients for a really special salad; or (2) Send Joe to the store with a detailed shopping list for salad materials. It all depends on how much faith the group has in Joe's knowledge, creativity, and sense of the occasion. The oral assignment (#1) may produce a true delight, should the store have some unusual vegetables that the group had not considered possibilities, and should Joe be clever enough to take advantage of the opportunity. The written assignment (#2) will produce a reasonable salad and avoid disaster, but at the same time it might force Joe to forgo the opportunity to make something especially exciting, should the store be well provided with unusual foods. Both assignments have their virtues, but they are based on opposite assumptions concerning the human factor, that is, Joe's ability to function in this situation.

In the same way, oral agreements depend a great deal on the reliability, imagination, knowledge, and perceptive powers of the parties involved. Written agreements leave far less to chance, but greatly inhibit future freedom of action at the same time.

The subtle metaphor: The difference between oral and written agreements more exactly parallels the difference between the knowledge we can have of a live person and that we can have of a literary character (a "written" person). Which can we "know" better? Which gives us more information?

On the one hand it may seem clear that we can know much more about the live person. We can learn so much from firsthand impressions (physical characteristics, behavior quirks and patterns, "vibrations") that is available to us only secondhand in a work of literature. Actually seeing blazing red hair strikes one differently than merely reading about it. Furthermore, the live person has infinite potential for complexity. Just when we think we know people they are likely to change their opinions, act out of character, or reveal hidden attributes we would have sworn they could not have possessed. Moreover, the vast expanses of future time bring with them unforeseen circumstances that may affect others so fundamentally that they become "different people." To add to all of this, the human psyche is so complex that no personality can be permanently delineated by an observer with complete confidence. The amount we can know about a live person, therefore, is infinite, seemingly much greater than that which can be known about a literary character, whose entire existence is limited to the words between the two covers of a book.

On the other hand, this concept of limitation allows us, in a different way, to know a great deal more about a literary character than we can ever know about a live person. In a sense, we can know a literary character completely, since everything that exists of the character can be found within the words on the pages before us. The character's actions are completely predictable; they will not change the next time we read the book. We need not concern ourselves with how the character might have acted in some situation not included in the book, since the character has no existence apart from that book. Hamlet, for example, was never twelve years old, because Shakespeare neither presents him nor talks about him at that age. Perhaps the knowledge we can have of a live person is infinite, ungraspable by any one human being; but the knowledge we can have of a literary character, because it is limited to the possibilities presented by the author's creation, is complete. It becomes a matter of semantics to decide which potential knowledge is greater.

In much the same way, an oral agreement, like the live person, can support infinite interpretations, while the written agreement limits the possibilities to the words which have expressed it.

With legal agreements we "reduce" the oral intentions to writing so that one at arm's-length may more easily deal with them, when that becomes necessary. The same happens when we have to deal from a distance with live persons (e.g., in deciding to strike up a conversation with a stranger or promote someone to lieutenant or admit a candidate to law school). We tend to "reduce" them to the status of literary characters by concentrating on them as the archetypes they resemble or by considering them as statistics, completed individuals who cannot change from their established identities, about whom everything can be known at one "reading." We pretend to know something about the stranger by his clothing or hair style or manner of speech. We might promote the soldier because of his record or refuse the would-be law student because she is forty years old. These people become easier to deal with if we reduce them from the live persons they are to the literary or "completed" characters we assume them to be. Indeed, if we did not imagine this metamorphosis, we would be stymied every time we had to deal with a person new to us. By the time we had finished trying to consider the infinite number of possibilities surrounding the identity or intentions or qualities of the newcomer, the moment of action would have passed us by. In the same way, courts cannot be expected to ponder endlessly the possible intentions behind an agreement, the possible pressures to act, the psychological advantages and disadvantages, and so forth. If a court has the parties' written agreement before it, it must limit its investigation to the literature it sees and not spend too much time pursuing the more inscrutable "live" intentions in the background.

The written agreement, then, is neither less than nor part of the original oral agreement, any more than a literary character is less than or part of a live person. The two have separate existences, even separate modes of existence. We do the written agreement and the literary character an injustice to think of them as "reduced" from their live counterparts. We ought to consider them intellectual creations that reflect, not reproduce, their models. The act of recording an agreement in words unavoidably changes the basic nature of the original sense of the agreement; what was a fluid, amoebic bundle of potential becomes a structured, articulated, completed statement. The writing has given to the infinite possibilities of the original intentions a form of existence that is in many ways both final and complete. The writing becomes an "instrument," whereas the intentions which produced it had only the potential for instrumentality. In essence, it matters much less what the parties might have thought than what the parties actually committed to paper. The latter might, and should, reflect the former accurately, but the two cannot be considered the same thing. You, as lawyer, might well be in touch with what your client wanted from a particular agreement, but if you are not aware of what else the words you produced can mean to an impartial reader, you have not adequately done your job.

You can develop precision by heightening your awareness of words and their powers. You can develop anti-precision by gaining experience in a given field, learning which things are likely to remain constant and which are likely to change with the passage of time. If you add to these an understanding of how a writing differs from the intentions which generated it, you will be prepared to write sound legal agreements. The task can be endlessly fascinating and yet almost equally annoying, for the problems continually change, and the pitfalls never completely disappear, no matter how expert you might become. The task of producing airtight expository prose can be awesome. The best we can hope to do is to minimalize the odds of possible misinterpretation. In most cases, that will suffice.

B.   BRIEFS

A brief is the written formal argument used in a court case. It normally includes a statement of facts, a defining of the relevant issues, and an argument, replete with references to previously decided cases supportive of the desired conclusion.

Under our Anglo-American legal system the decision-making process at the trial court level is broken down into three distinct functions: It is the job of the jury to discern and establish the facts of the case (although some trials proceed without a jury, in which case the judge assumes this function); it is the job of the judge to sift the legal arguments, apply them to the facts, and make substantive and procedural decisions; and it is the job of the lawyers (called "counsel" in this situation) to make the best possible arguments for their clients, first in written form (the brief), to be submitted before the trial, and then in oral form, delivered during the trial. In a court of appeals the same roles pertain except that there is no need for a fact finder (like the jury), the facts having been established permanently in the lower court.

Only three of the five modes of discourse are used in writing a brief: Narration, Exposition, and Persuasion. The statement of facts must be purely narrative, excluding all opinions, inferences, and interpretations. The lawyer's opportunity to opine, infer, and interpret comes in the defining of the issues, a task of Exposition. The main body of the brief is given over to Persuasion, as the lawyer tries to convince the court to accept the prior definition of issues and agree with the suggested conclusions. Descriptive writing plays little or no part in a brief because it matters little to the court how the lawyer felt about or reacted to the situation at hand. Argumentation is set aside here in favor of Persuasion. It is not for the lawyer to judge what is "truth" (which is the goal of Argumentation): That is the responsibility of the judge. The lawyer is called upon only to present the best case possible, to try to demonstrate that his theory is more persuasive than the opposite side's. (Please note: Despite the distinction between the modes of Persuasion and Argumentation, we freely refer to the lawyer's attempts at persuasion as "arguments." Our lack of another more appropriate term confuses the issue a bit, here.)

Any overlapping of modes of discourse in your brief will weaken the total effect it should have and leave you open to attack by your adversary. Conversely, any overlapping on your adversary's part should give you a strong base for refutation of his or her arguments. For example, if a lawyer introduces expository writing into the narration of facts, it often means that he or she feels that the facts, stated by themselves, would appear to be more favorable for the other side. The same applies to the introduction of Persuasion into the expository defining of the issues. If the lawyer cannot wait for the proper time to make the convincing argument, then the lawyer probably does not trust the appearance given by the issues objectively defined. Both overlappings are signs of weakness, a fear that the court will jump to a seemingly all too obvious conclusion, for the other side.

When you find yourself exhibiting these signs of weakness ("danger signals" on a larger scale), let it be a warning to you that subconsciously you have not the confidence in your case that you ought to have. It may lead you to straighten out your own thinking before the judge or your opponent has the chance to straighten it out for you, to the detriment of your client.

Conversely, when you spot this kind of overlapping in your opponent's brief, continue to prod the surface until you find the weak spot that you can assume to be there. The process will reveal to you precisely what worries your opponent the most. It will not be enough for you to accuse the opposite side of mixing up its modes of discourse. You must use the mixup as a clue to discover the weakness that bred it. You can use your opponent's weak verbs in the same way (see Chapter II).

C. MEMOS

"Memo" is an abbreviation for "memorandum," a Latin word meaning "that which must be remembered." Memos can vary in length from a few sentences to several pages and are written either at the request of a colleague (often senior to the writer) or for inclusion in the file that contains all the business transacted for a client.

In the former case, the requester of the memo usually wants to be fully informed about a specific point of law that will affect the well being of the client. The lawyer writing the memo must research what is already known and then suggest as many different perspectives on the subject as are reasonable. Instead of limiting a legal relationship (the job of an agreement) or making a persuasive argument (the job of a brief), the writer must in this case present the subject from multiple points of view. Using the information in the memo, the senior person can make intelligent decisions about which courses of action to pursue. Memo writing, therefore, requires extreme clarity, objectivity, and an ability to see issues from many perspectives.

One writes a memo for a file to record for future readers of the file all the events, thoughts, or moments of understanding that might be pertinent to the client's affairs. Since the writer of the memo will not know who will be reading the memo in the future or under what conditions, he or she must attempt to achieve yet a greater degree of thoroughness than that for the former kind of memo, while still requiring the same clarity, objectivity, and perspicacity.

A lawyer must call upon all five modes of discourse in writing memos. The more formal and extensive the memo, the larger number of modes will probably be called for. Narrative prose will be used for the stating of facts. Description, so out of place in an agreement or brief, plays an important role here, as the lawyer's personal responses, reactions, and senses often prove significant in explaining the situation to a reader unfamiliar with the case. Exposition often dominates memos as the lawyer makes a record of what he or she thought about the situation at critical moments. Argumentation may be used in the search for the truth of the issue, and Persuasion in the search for the most convincing arguments possible.

Memo writers must be careful not to succumb to the temptation to write for themselves as their primary audience. It is then that crucial terms are left unexplained, significant facts are left unstated, and conclusions appear without the benefit of the logical steps that produced them. Most of the time a memo writer should be addressing one of two audiences, either a reader who knows a great deal about the client and the situation (in which case the memo can be concise and specific) or a reader who knows nothing whatever of the whole affair (in which case the memo should be thorough, explanatory, and general as well as specific). The latter audience demands a completeness beyond that which you might have the patience (or time) to produce. In these cases you should take several deep breaths, remember how important detail and thoroughness have been in so many other situations, and somehow find the energy to persevere. Not only will others benefit when they read your full account of the matter, but you yourself, returning to the file some years later, will be gratified to find a clear account of previous events and thoughts, long after you had forgotten about them.

D. LETTERS TO CLIENTS

Letters to clients deal mostly with the definition of some part of a legal situation (what has been done, what can be done, what is being done, what ought to be done, etc.). Like memos, they utilize all five modes of discourse, all for similar reasons. It is only the sense of audience that distinguishes letter writing from memo writing. Each client represents a different audience for the lawyer, and it takes a keen sensitivity to the needs and personality of the client to produce just the right tone, the right level of erudition, and the right extent of detail necessary.

In letters to the clients lawyers are severely tempted to resort to Legalese, that puffing up of language with jargon and redundancies that has so typified legal writing in the past and has helped to sully the profession's reputation. The main causes of Legalese, some of which were suggested in Chapter I, are all invidious:

(1) Some lawyers want to sound like lawyers, especially when they are talking law, and they fear if they use "Plain English" they will seem unprofessional, even incompetent;

(2) Some want to give clients the impression that without the lawyer to interpret and communicate in Legalese, the client would be lost in a verbal jungle and fall prey to any of a number of predators;

(3) Some fear that if they do not sound professional their clients will balk at paying them such high wages; some even believe that the public demands the fancy language as part of the price it pays;

(4) Some feel that keeping their profession a mystery will protect and increase the public's dependence on them;

(5) Some are fooled into thinking that pomposity of tone represents depth of thought; and

(6) Some have never learned to express themselves clearly and succinctly.

The negative concept of Legalese does not include the proper use of "terms of art," legal terminology which has been precisely defined to serve specific legal purposes. A certain amount of specialized language is necessary in a profession that spends so much of its time defining and redefining words so that we will have symbols for the concepts that affect us. None of these special needs, however, can justify the random insertions of "heretofore mentioned" and the transmogrifications of "phone call" into "telephonic communication." Put those two together and see what verbal depravity can do: "That phone call" becomes "the heretofore mentioned telephonic communication." Using language like that in private communication eventually leads to using language like that of the following constitutional amendment addressed to the public, at which point private wrongs have become public disasters.

> No moneys derived from any fees, excises, or license taxes, levied by the state, relating to registration, operation, or use of vehicles upon the public highways except a vehicle-use tax imposed in lieu of a sales tax, and no moneys derived from any fee, excises, or license taxes, levied by the state, relating to fuels used for propelling such vehicles except pump taxes, shall be used for other than cost of administering such laws, statutory refunds and adjustments allowed therein, cost of construction, reconstruction, maintenance and rights-of-way, payment of highway obligations, the cost of traffic regulation, and the expense of enforcing state traffic and motor vehicle laws.[1]

Would you vote yea or nay?

Letters to clients should be kept as direct and simple as the occasion allows. All the arguments listed above in favor of Legalese are arguments from weakness. No lawyer in control of his or her professional skills need fear being underestimated, underpayed, or underneeded. Lawyers should act as the guardians of exact language, not as the perverters of it.

EXERCISE

Hypothetical: Part 1

Your client, Sam Aritan, wishes to give some direction to the life of his headstrong, irresponsible, rather greedy niece, Willa. He is convinced that a college education will help "straighten her out," but Willa has resisted the suggestion. Sam has decided to play upon her greed for her own good and wants to offer Willa the following deal: If she will go to college for four years and get a Bachelor's degree, he will give her $20,000 on the day of her graduation and leave her $150,000 in his will.

---

1. Quoted in James C. Raymond, "Legal Writing: An Obstruction to Justice," *Alabama Law Review*, XXX (1978), p. 3.

Task #1

Draft the agreement for Sam. Consider carefully how much of his intentions should be articulated.

Hypothetical: Part 2

Willa is enticed by the money and signs the agreement. She then enrolls in Alma Mater University, a correspondence school she read about on a match book cover. For four years she takes course after course, doing little work and sending in short, careless assignments. AMU, happy to have her as a continuing source of income, gives her straight A's. At the end of four years she receives a B.A. in the mail. Sam is furious and refuses to give her the $20,000 or include her in his will. Willa sues Sam.

Task #2

Draft a brief for Sam's side of the case, stating the facts, defining the issues, and making the best argument you can, but omitting all legal research. Work only from your native logical powers.

Hypothetical: Part 3

Your firm suddenly decides to transfer you to another city for at least two years. Someone else, whom you do not know, will be taking over Sam's case.

Task #3

Write a memo to the file about the entire business so that anyone who succeeds you will understand the situation clearly.

Hypothetical: Part 4

Just before you leave, Sam pleads with you to write two letters, one to Willa's attorney and one to Willa herself, in an attempt to settle the case before it comes to court.

Task #4

Write the two letters.

Task #5

Looking back over the first four tasks (which comprise writings to five different audiences), try to articulate what effect your sense of audience had on the way you chose to write each one. How did your style differ, and why? How did the content differ, and why? How did you feel about writing each, and why? Which was the easiest to write, which the hardest, and why? Which is your best writing, which your worst, and why?

Chapter VI

READING WHAT'S THERE: INSTRUCTIONS, INFERENCES, AND FACTS

This chapter focusses on the difficulty of attaining absolute precision in writing even of straightforward narration. It asks you to do some extremely critical reading, subjecting rather minute details to a scrutiny that may seem excessive to any but lawyers, lawmakers, and philosophers.

We will deal with three topics:

(A) Instructions: How to communicate in writing the best way to do something;

(B) Inferences: How to recognize the distinction between what a narrative says and what it only seems to say;

(C) Statements of Fact: How to establish what is agreed upon as having happened.

We cover these topics for two main reasons. (1) Most of the writing done by lawyers must eventually stand on its own, unaided by any oral explanation by the writer of what was "actually" intended. Recognizing ambiguity or failure of communication in your own writing is a remarkably tricky task, necessitating much practice and almost constant vigilance. Learning how to spot the errors and inconsistencies in other's writing will make the self-correction process easier and more effective. (2) Often lawyers are faced with the task of discovering what is wrong or inconsistent in someone else's written work. The particular details singled out in this chapter for criticism may sometimes appear to you meticulously or even frivolously chosen, but they strictly parallel the kinds of details you will be asked to deal with in actual practice.

A. INSTRUCTIONS

Instructions are narrative writings that tell the reader how to perform some task or attain some goal. Their effectiveness can be judged by two different kinds of tests: (1) Have you successfully completed the task or attained the goal once you have followed them? (2) How difficult were they to understand and to follow? The first test is one of action, necessarily involving the process we call "trial and error." Since lawyers prefer to minimalize the possibilities of "error" in their work, we shall concentrate on the second test, the process of intellectual judgment.

Good instructions comprise five qualities:

(1) Sound logic (which includes a meaningful ordering of steps);

(2) Completeness;

(3) Clarity of expression (which includes precision of vocabulary);

(4) Consistency; and

(5) Sensitivity to audience (which includes appropriateness of tone).

A lack of any one of these might cause the instructions to fail in their communicative task.

The importance of the first four qualities should be evident, but it may come as something of a surprise to realize that the most logical, complete, clear, and consistent instructions can fail if they are aimed too high or too low for their audience. Too little information will leave the novice in a quandary; too much information can obscure the relative importance of details even for the most experienced. Use of the wrong tone can antagonize any reader into paying too little attention.

The following is a set of instructions on how to change a bicycle wheel. How good are they?

[(cl) means clockwise, and usually tightens a nut or bolt. (c-cl) means counterclockwise, and usually loosens a bolt.]

10. Ten speed people, work your wheel axle into the drop-outs, slipping the chain over the smallest sprocket. Seat both axles all the way into the ends of the drop-out slots and tighten (cl) the nuts. Keeping the right end of the axle firmly seated, slide the left end slightly forward until the front of the wheel is centered (aligned) between the two chain stays. With the wheel in exactly this position, tighten (cl) the nuts up well against the frame.

1, 3, 10. One speed, three speed, and ten speed people, whichever kind of rear wheel you have replaced, tighten up the brakes (1 speed people, re-attach the brake arm to the frame).

To replace a *front wheel with a bolt-on axle or wing nuts*, spin (c-cl) the nuts until they're near the ends of the axle, then work the axle all the way into the drop-outs. Tighten (cl) both nuts with your fingers, then make sure both ends of the wheel axle are still seated all the way against the tops of the drop-out slots. Check the alinement by seeing if the rim of the wheel is equidistant from each of the fork arms. If it's really off, like rubbing against one of the fork arms, your forks are really bent. Now tighten (cl) the axle nuts well with a wrench. If tightening one nut turns the whole axle, use a wrench on each nut. Recheck the alinement, reset your brakes if they were released, and you are set to go.

We can judge the effectiveness of these instructions by testing them for the five qualities enumerated above.

(1) Sound logic (which includes a meaningful ordering of steps). Does each of these steps make sense to you? Do they progress logically one to the other? Can you even begin to judge the logic, given your knowledge of bicycles?

(2) Completeness. Is there anything omitted that you particularly need to know? Can you judge completeness without actually doing the process described?

(3) Clarity of expression (which includes precision of vocabulary). Do you have any problems with his sentence structure? Are there many words which breed confusion? For example, in the third paragraph we read, "make sure both ends of the wheel axle are still seated all the way against the tops of the drop-out slots." What does the word "seated" imply? When something is "seated all the way," is it usually found "against the top" of something? What visual image does this raise for you? Is this a problem that might be cleared up by the experience of doing the action in question?

(4) Consistency. Does the writer lack consistency in his technical terms or in his use of common language? In the second sentence of the first paragraph we are told to "tighten (cl) the

nuts"; and yet two sentences later we are asked to "tighten (cl) the [same] nuts up well." Does this imply that whenever we are told merely to "tighten," we should do it as impermanently as possible? What if we had tightened the nuts securely as a response to the instruction of the second sentence?

(5) Sensitivity to audience (which includes appropriateness of tone). Has this writer clearly decided for whom he is writing? Sometimes he treats us as if we were reasonably experienced, sometimes like beginners. For instance, in the second paragraph we are assumed to know exactly how to "tighten up the brakes," for we are told to do so without further comment; but at the end of the third paragraph we are assumed to know little about the art of tightening, for as we are told to "tighten (cl) the axle nuts well with a wrench," we are also cautioned that "if tightening one nut turns the whole axle, use a wrench on each nut."

Another example: We find no explanation for words like "drop-outs," "sprocket," "chain stays," "brake arm," and "fork arms": Yet at the same time we find a definition for "aligned" ("center-ed") and one for "really off" ("like rubbing against one of the fork arms"). Is there an audience that would have no need for the former terms to be defined yet still need the latter?

Do you have difficulty with the change in tone throughout? At times it seems quite formal and business-like, rather "at arm's length": "Check the alignment by seeing if the rim of the wheel is equidistant from each of the fork arms." More often, however, he adopts an "arm around the shoulder" tone, calling us by familiarized titles like "ten speed people" and using personal possessives ("work *your* wheel axle into the drop-outs"), dismissing us at the end with a pat on the back ("and you are set to go"). In what way and by how much does this confusion of tone affect the audience's ability to follow the instructions? What impression does it give you of the author? Would you buy another "how-to" book by him.

To be sensitive to an audience, then, a writer must make firm decisions about whom the audience comprises, how they expect to be spoken to, and how much they need to be told. The writer should adopt a tone that reflects these decisions and maintain it consistently throughout.

EXERCISE

Criticize thoroughly the following instructions for the packing and shipping of a phonograph turntable, listing both strengths and weaknesses for each of the five categories used above.

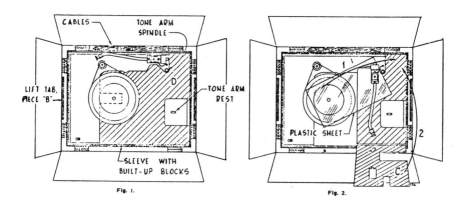

Fig. 1.   Fig. 2.

PACKING AND SHIPPING OF THE
XF–683 TURNTABLE

1. Open the top flaps of the carton and remove all the inner pieces except the large flat sections at the bottom with die-cut holes for the outer platter and accessories. *Do not* return the outer platter and accessories if you are sending the turntable for repairs.

2. (a) Remove the dust cover from the turntable. (b) Remove the record mat and the outer section of the platter. (c) Remove the cartridge shell. (d) Loosen the brass counterweight set screw, slide the counterweight to the front as far as it will go, and retighten the set screw.

3. Center the turntable base approximately on packing piece B (the one with lift tabs), and drape the power cord and amplifier cable out to the back.

4. Apply a piece of masking tape over our emblem on the front edge of the base. Then slide the large wrap-around sleeve, with the built-up cardboard blocks, gently over and around the wooden

turntable base. Push the sleeve down until it stops against packing piece B.

5. Lift the front end of the tone arm out of the tone arm rest. Slide packing piece D to the left over the tone arm rest and under the inner platter until it will rest flat against the turntable top plate (see Fig. 1).

6. Unscrew the tone arm spindle from the tone arm completely, and lay the tone arm along the back edge of the turntable top plate, with the flat section down. BE CAREFUL not to strain the tone arm wiring. DO NOT remove the tone arm spindle from its bearing well.

7. Unfold packing piece C and lay the bottom part in place over packing piece D and just inside the right-hand edge of the outer sleeve. Put the piece of clear plastic sheet over the rectangular cutout in piece C, with most of the plastic extending to the left (see Fig. 2). Then lay the tone arm, upside down, in its cutout in piece C and over the plastic sheet. Fold the plastic sheet over the rectangular section of the tone arm and over the top of the tone arm spindle, and then fold the other half of packing piece C over the tone arm and spindle. Be sure that the back edge of the counterweight projects through the upper half of packing piece C.

8. Lift this entire assembly by the tabs on packing piece B. Holding the wrap-around sleeve down against packing piece B with your thumbs, and taking care that the cables do not get *under* piece B, ease the assembly into the carton and onto the accessories tray. Pack the cables between the outer carton and the back edge of the sleeve.

9. Packing piece A should be prepared by inserting the four tabs into slots at the ends of the bottom, and bending the tabs to hold them in the slots. The end flaps should then be folded up and piece A put in the carton so that the *record* spindle goes up through the small hole at center left. Repeat: *The record spindle must come through the hole in the bottom of packing piece A.* Push packing piece A down firmly when the spindle is seated in the hole.

Lawyers constantly find themselves writing instructions, not about mechanical procedures, but about intellectual procedures.

They instruct people how to think about a situation and how to do something about it. These concerns dominate three of the four forms of writing a lawyer confronts (briefs, agreements, and letters, memos only being excepted).

In a brief, the lawyer attempts to instruct the court how to view the situation before it and how to reason its way to the "correct" decision. In doing this, the lawyer must concentrate on qualities (1) and (2) above, soundness of logic and completeness. Any false step or missing step in the reasoning process can prove fatal to the case.

In writing an agreement, the lawyer stresses qualities (3) and (4), clarity of expression and consistency. Since an agreement usually attempts to define a relationship, the text of it must instruct all parties involved how to think about themselves, how to think about others, what they must do, what they must refrain from doing, and what they will have to do in case of a breach. Ambiguity or inconsistency here has often caused courts to void the whole agreement.

In writing letters (to clients or to those with whom the clients are dealing), the lawyer must concentrate on quality (5), sensitivity to audience. All of the other qualities are necessary, to be sure, but understanding of and sensitivity to audience should override all other considerations. The most brilliant legal advice will be diminished in its effect, perhaps even wasted entirely, if aimed too high or too low, too intimately or too coldly, too respectfully or too irreverently.

You will probably find that dealing with legal instructions, especially the dictates of government bureaucracies, will result in headaches for you, either physical or metaphorical, throughout your professional and personal lives. Whenever possible, people tend to hire professionals (lawyers, CPA's, real estate agents, architects) to deal with these forms for them. If you wish to understand why, try filling out your own income tax forms this year (avoiding the short form). Even better, fill "them" out (for practice only) for a creation of your imagination who owns stocks and bonds, has sold real estate in the taxable year, whose business functions on a buy-now-pay-later basis, and who purchases large amounts of depreciable machinery every year.

EXERCISE

Cities usually zone their land according to potential use, thereby maintaining control over the development of the character of individual neighborhoods.   In some zones, for instance, they might permit highrise apartments, while limiting buildings to three stories in others.   They might allow commercial buildings in one area while restricting another area to residential buildings.   In order to build a structure disallowed by the zoning restrictions in a certain area, an individual must apply to the Zoning Board for a "variance," showing good cause why the forbidden building should be allowed as an exceptional case.   The following document is an actual Notice of Zoning Appeal used by one of the fastest growing cities in the United States.   This document is intended to instruct people how to structure an appeal.

Thoroughly criticize this document as an instructional form. You might use the five qualities as before for your organization, or you might proceed linearly through the form itself, making multiple comments as you go.   In either case, be as thorough as you can.

Then rewrite the document, assuming whatever knowledge you need to to make it meaningful and complete.   Do not look up other cities' Notices.   The purpose of the exercise is for you to undergo the rewriting process, not for you to "get the right answer."

Notice of Zoning Appeal

TO THE BOARD OF ADJUSTMENT UNDER THE ZONING ORDINANCE OF FASTGRO CITY AND TO THE BUILDING INSPECTOR OF FASTGRO CITY:

Please note that _____ the owner, hereby appeals to the Board of Adjustment of Fastgro City from the order of the Building Inspector dated _____ denying a permit to erect _____ at _____ which is in a _____ zoning district.
official address

Existing use of the premises _____

Will this addition or remodelling change the use? _____

If so, how? _____

The proposed construction does not meet the requirements of the zoning ordinance of Fastgro City in the following respects:

_____

Said petitioner contends that the requested variance should be granted due to the following:

(Under State law the following conditions must be shown to exist before the Board of Adjustment has the power to grant a variance.)

1. The granting of the variance will not be contrary to the public interest and the literal enforcement of the provisions of the zoning ordinance will result in unnecessary hardships and the spirit and intent of the zoning ordinance will be upheld due to the following facts: _____

_____

_____

2. The variance will not substantially affect the comprehensive plan of zoning in the city and unless a variance is granted, difficulties and hardships will be imposed upon the applicant which are unnecessary to carry out the purpose of the plan due to the following conditions: _____

_____

_____

_____

3. The following special circumstances are attached to the property covered by this petition which do not generally apply to other property in the same district and because of these special circumstances the owner is being deprived of a substantial property right possessed by other property in the same district: _____

_____

_____

Additional Information Required

One PLOT PLAN, to be attached hereto, which is:

A drawing of the lot to be built upon, showing the actual dimensions thereof, the size and location of any existing buildings and proposed buildings (including new additions to existing building) and the plan and location of off-street parking facilities. Also indicate the distance to the nearest dwellings on all abutting properties. An original drawing or duplicate print, not smaller than 8½″ × 11″, will be acceptable. INCOMPLETE OR OTHERWISE UNREADABLE DRAWINGS WILL BE REFUSED.

Refusal of drawings may result in a delayed hearing before the Board.

An elevation.

If building is to be constructed on property line or if there is a dispute on property line location, a survey is required.

Furnish NAMES and MAILING ADDRESSES of all owners of property abutting and across the street; also any other property affected: _____

_____

_____

_____

Furnish LEGAL DESCRIPTION of lot: _____

_____

_____

_____

INSTRUCTIONS:

FILING INFORMATION:

File completed application (plot plan and elevation included) with:

Department of Building and Housing Services
Room 214, City & County Building
Fastgro City

The FILING FEE required is $20.00 (twenty dollars). No petition will be considered unless this fee is paid.

NOTE: It is required that each case up for hearing will be presented and argued before the Board of Adjustment either by the Petitioner or by an authorized agent. If represented by an agent, the agent must have written authorization from the owner.

GENERAL INFORMATION

The Fastgro City Board of Adjustment meets in session once or twice each month. The exact dates for these meetings are determined from the number of requests received. Please phone 757–7823 for information regarding these dates and the deadline for filing. State law requires that all petitions for variances must be advertised by the Board at least one week before a scheduled meeting.

All variances will be recorded.

———◆———

Chapter IV of this book dealt with the definition of words and concepts. This chapter continues that topic, for a set of instructions is no more nor less than a definition of a process. When a judge gives instructions to the members of a jury, she explains the Law for them and proscribes the boundaries of their deliberations, thereby defining the process they are to follow in coming to their decision. When a government instructs the public through legislation or through the requirements of administrative forms, it is defining processes which directly affect the possibilities of action of the public. Sometimes the nature of the language used to communicate instructions can even raise serious social and moral problems. Some states, for example, use questionnaire forms that run to fifteen or twenty pages to qualify people for receiving food stamps (part of welfare programing). If the language, length, and complexity of these forms so intimidate the people who are intended to use them that they despair of being able to respond correctly, the forms deny *de facto* the very aid they were created to provide. The following exercise will give you an opportunity to tussle with this kind of problem.

EXERCISE

The lengthy excerpt that follows represents approximately one quarter of the "Application for Status as a Permanent Resident" form used by the United States Department of Justice, Immigration, and Naturalization Service. A great majority of the people who must respond to these instructions do not know English well and may never have dealt directly with governmental authority before. Failure to comply with the instructions would result in a severe penalty, the disallowance of American residency.

Read the instructions carefully. Then, in as much detail as possible, respond to the following:

(1) What are the specific ambiguities and obscurities that must be dealt with by the applicant?

(2) What, if anything, is "unfair" about the form?

(3) How could problems with the form be resolved by rewriting and revising?

Then rewrite two substantial passages, clarifying and simplifying as much as you can, keeping the concept of audience in mind at all times.

Application for Status as a Permanent Resident

Issued by the United States Department of Justice,
Immigration and Naturalization Service

INSTRUCTIONS

Read Instructions carefully. Fee will not be refunded.

1. **APPLICATION.** A separate application must be executed by each applicant. An application in behalf of a child under 14 years of age shall be executed by the parent or guardian. Also, unless you checked box "B" of block 1, you must complete and submit with this application a Form SS–5. Application for Social Security Number, regardless of your age and regardless of whether you already have a social security account number. Form G–325A (Biographic Information) must be completed and submitted with each application if the applicant is 14 years of age or older. Failure to do so delays action and may result in return of the application.

2. **FEE.** A fee of twenty-five dollars ($25) must be paid for filing this application. If your application is rejected on the ground that it is not considered to have been properly filed because of failure to submit a labor certification if required (see Instruction 10), or because a visa number is not available, fee may be refunded. Otherwise, the fee cannot be refunded regardless of the action taken on the application. **DO NOT MAIL CASH.**

ALL FEES MUST BE SUBMITTED IN THE EXACT AMOUNT. Payment by check or money order must be drawn on a bank or other institution located in the United States and be payable in United States currency. If you reside in the Virgin Islands, check or money order must be payable to the "Commissioner of Finance of the Virgin Islands." If you reside in Guam, check or money order must be payable to the "Treasurer, Guam." All other applicants must make the check or money order payable to the "Immigration and Naturalization Service." When check is drawn on an account of a person other than the applicant, the name of the applicant must be entered on the face of the check. If payment is made by the type of international money order that cannot be mailed, the money order must be drawn on the postmaster of the city of the United States to which the application will be mailed, and that city, the money order number, and the date must be shown clearly on the top margin of the application form.

3. **PHOTOGRAPHS.** Except in the case of an applicant under fourteen years of age, you must submit with this application two photographs of yourself taken within 30 days of the date of this application. These photographs must be 1½ by 1½ inches in size, and the distance from the top of head to point of chin should be approximately 1¼ inches. They must not be pasted on cards or mounted in any way, must be on thin paper, have a light background, and clearly show a front view of your face without a hat. Snapshots, group, full-length portraits or vending machine photographs will not be accepted. Using crayon or soft pencil to avoid possible mutilation of the photographs, write your name lightly on the reverse of the photographs.

4. **FINGERPRINTS.** A completed fingerprint card (Form FD–258) must be submitted by each applicant who is 14 years of age or older. Fingerprint cards with instructions for their completion are available at any office of the Immigration and Naturalization Service. You may have your fingerprints recorded on Form FD–258 at an office of this Service or you may prefer to present Form FD–258 at a police station or sheriff's office and request an officer there to record your fingerprints on the card. The card must be signed by you in the presence of the officer taking your fingerprints, who must then sign his name and enter

the date in the spaces provided. It is important to furnish all the information called for on the card.

5. DOCUMENTS.

a. *General.* All documents must be submitted in the original. If you desire to have the original of any of the other documents returned, and if copies are by law permitted to be made, you may submit photographic or typewritten copies. If you submit copies, the original documents must be presented at the time of your examination. Each foreign document must be accompanied by a translation certified by the translator as to the accuracy of the translation and as to his competency to translate. If you are unable to secure documentary evidence from abroad, you must submit proof of the efforts you have made to secure such documents.

b. *Submit the following documents only if you checked box "A" or "D" in block 1 of the application.*

(1) Record of your birth.

(2) A letter from your present employer showing employment of a permanent nature, if you are employed, or an affidavit or support Form I–134 from a responsible person in the United States, or other evidence to establish that you are not likely to become a public charge.

(3) If you are the spouse or unmarried child of a person who has been granted preference classification by the Immigration and Naturalization Service or has applied for preference classification, and you are claiming the same preference classification, or if you are claiming special immigrant classification as the spouse or unmarried child of a minister of religion who has been accorded or is seeking classification as a special immigrant, submit the following: *For the spouse:* Marriage certificate and proof of termination of all prior marriages of each spouse. *For the child:* Marriage certificate of parents, together with proof of termination of their prior marriages, if such documents have not been submitted by a parent.

(4) . . .

(5) . . .

c. . . .

d. . . .

(1) Examples of documents which may be submitted to prove residence are: .   .   .

NOTE: Women unemployed since marriage and unable to furnish evidence in their own names may furnish evidence in the names of their parents or other persons with whom they have been living if affidavits of the parents or other persons are submitted attesting to residence with them.   If any of the documents are lengthy or bulky, only the pertinent parts should be attached.

B.   INFERENCES

We have noted previously the distinction between obscurity (a lack of clarity in meaning) and ambiguity (multiple possibilities of meaning).   Now we deal with inferences, a relative of these two language demons.   An inference is a meaning, based on likelihood, suggestion, or association, that does not appear explicitly in the author's words.   These three demons each have a different effect on a reader.   Obscurity makes it impossible for a reader to divine any meaning whatever from the author's words.   Ambiguity either confuses the reader with its multiple choices or camouflages the author's intended meaning with the other possibilities.   Inference causes the reader to fill in information or thought not explicitly stated, thereby effecting a kind of revision of the author's text.

The "facts" we infer many times each day most often prove consistent with actuality.   For example: When we see a police car, with sirens whining and lights flashing, force to the side of a highway a sports car travelling at high speed, we normally infer that: (1) The driver of the sports car was breaking the law by exceeding the speed limit;   (2) the police car contains a police officer, who has stopped the sports car for speeding;   and (3) a lecture, warning, or speeding ticket will result.   Probably our analysis is correct;   but several other explanations for these conditions and events are also possible.

Alternative #1:   The police stopped the sports car, which was travelling at the maximum allowable speed, because it was not displaying a rear license plate.

Alternative #2:   The driver of the sports car was the Police Commissioner, who was on his way home having left behind at the office his anniversary gift for his wife. The officer in the police car had been ordered to get the gift to the Commissioner before he reached home.

Alternative #3: The drivers of both cars were in the process of committing a robbery together. The man in the sports car had heisted the loot, and the woman in the car disguised as a police car was to take it from him and transport it at high speed over the state line.

The urge to infer is a compulsive one, stemming from many possible sources. Like the cat who is always on the wrong side of a closed door, we constantly want to know all about the mystery that is just out of reach. We have been raised to provide answers for everything, and the scientific and technological advances of the Twentieth Century have suggested to some of us that answers are always a possibility. Answers make us feel comfortable, feel superior. If we understand everything from a god's-eye view, then we can avoid feeling threatened by others. Conversely, we sense that ignorance breeds weakness and leaves us less in charge of our lives. Perhaps this accounts in part for our great delight in the novels, movies, and television shows which allow us to know the innermost thoughts of all the main characters; god-like we survey the scene, all-powerful, unassailable in our perfect knowledge. It is the most comfortable and comforting of situations.

Along with these rather defensive motives, perhaps our natural creative urges also help to induce us to make inferences. Once our attention is attracted (e.g., by a police car chasing a sports car), our imagination delights in dwelling on the subject, filling in details so that in a sense we help to create (and thereby control) the situation. We do this every time we finish a book or a movie if we continue to let the characters live on in our mind, having further adventures beyond those created by the author. A Nineteenth Century writer, Mary Cowden Clarke, overindulged this urge by writing a series of best-selling stories called *The Girlhood of Shakespeare's Heroines,* in which she surmised what Juliet and others were like at the age of ten, what Ophelia thought of Hamlet before the gloom of Act I, Scene i had descended upon him.

We can make inferences safely when dealing with situations that do not involve us directly (police arresting sporty speeders, fictitious characters struggling with their even more fictitious adolescences); but when writings have immediate effects on us (contracts for services or sales of goods, employment agreements, insurance policies), the fictionalizing process of inference can prove disastrous.

An inference is a conclusion based not on logic but on probability. In relying upon it, a writer accepts "it seems to me" as the equivalent of "it is demonstrated to be."

Picture it this way. A series of stepping-stones span a river. The bank upon which you stand represents the logical premises of your argument; the far bank represents your wished-for conclusion; the stepping-stones represent the logical steps of argumentation by which you move from premises to conclusion. You start across. Midway you come upon a dark swirl of water which appears to be covering a stone you would use for your next step: It is the dark shadow of Inference. You cannot be sure that a stepping-stone lurks underneath the swirling waters, but both Probability and Convenience, the chief supporters of Inference, urge you forward. If you trust in Inference, one of two things will happen: If you are lucky and there actually is a stone there, you can proceed without interruption towards your conclusion; if not, you will sink into the waters of Confusion, your argument will be destroyed and your journey end in disaster.

One can sometimes rely on inferences without adversely affecting the strength of an argument; but since we cannot distinguish clearly between safe inferences and dangerous ones, it is better to avoid them altogether. Such false steps, even when they do not make you slip, will make others unwilling to follow you with confidence.

These warnings against the acceptance of inference may seem to imply that we should place our reliance only on fact or truth; yet many a philosopher will argue against the existence of an objective reality, whether called "fact," "truth," or anything else. While these arguments might (and perhaps should) fascinate lawyers, no final decision on their validity is necessary for the competent practice of law. Within certain restrictions, the parties to a contractual agreement can conclude between themselves what they choose to accept as "fact" and act on it accordingly. In a court of law, "fact" is "determined" by the jury (or by the judge, in a juryless trial): Whatever the "finder of fact" concludes is accepted as actual fact for purposes of the trial, and even a court of appeal is bound by those findings.

"Truth" is often defined in law as that which seems most probable, and not as that which is objectively identifiable as uncontestable. The Law, whether publicly legislated or privately agreed upon, exists to be used, not merely to be pondered. Parties to an agreement cannot wait until their dealings are completed to decide what would have been the most equitable way of arranging matters; they must define their parameters and take their chances. Courts cannot delay their decisions until certainty has surfaced; they must act on what seems most "reasonable" and hope justice results.

"The best argument becomes accepted as Truth." To combat the misuse of such an alarming concept, we have established legal procedures and standards that are intended to protect and encourage, as best they can, the system's natural tendency towards "truth." The rules of Evidence, for example, allow witnesses to testify only to what they saw, heard, said, or did, not to what they might infer from those experiences. Alleged criminals do not become actual criminals until a jury is convinced "beyond a reasonable doubt" that the defendant is guilty. If "truth" is only a probability, then the least we can do is prevent the geometric increase of uncertainty that would be caused by allowing further probabilities (inferences) to help determine the central probability ("truth").

We try to unearth the hardest core of actuality we know (what the words of a contract actually are, what the witness actually saw, what the defendant actually said), knowing that at best we will still be dealing only in extreme possibilities. Inferences are especially treacherous because they sound so "safe" that they lull us into comfortable beliefs of certainty.

Any good lawyer can distinguish an inference from a reasonable conclusion at a glance and can use that logical gap to destroy the seeming coherence of an opponent's argument. Inference, by definition, always covers up a spot of "reasonable doubt." A good lawyer should also be able to spot inference-gaps in his or her own arguments. With practice one can become adept at inference spotting. Here, then, is some practice.

An Inference Test

Read the following narrative carefully, accepting all of it as true. Then label each of the 25 statements that follow as either "True," "False," or "?". "True" means that the statement can be absolutely verified by the information given in the narrative. "False" means that the statement can be absolutely disproved by the information given in the narrative. "?" means that the statement could be either true or false, given the information in the narrative.

The answers, with explanations appear directly after the list of questions. Do your best to ignore the answers until after you have decided upon your own.

Narrative

The owner of a restaurant had just unlocked the front door when a man wearing a hat appeared and demanded money from the woman at the cash register. Words were exchanged, and the man became excited. The cash register was opened, its contents scooped up, and the man sped away with the money he had demanded, leaving his hat behind. A member of the police force, who had been telephoned immediately, came, discussed the matter, took the hat, and drove off.

Statements

(1) Four people were involved in the story.

(2) Only one woman was involved in the story.

(3) Three women were involved in the story.

(4) The robbery took place at the cash register.

(5) The incident did not take place at the end of the business day.

(6) The owner of the restaurant was present during the incident.

(7) The owner unlocked the front door from the inside.

(8) The man who owned the restaurant unlocked the front door.

(9) The owner unlocked the front door of the restaurant.

(10) A man wearing a hat entered by the door that the owner had just unlocked.

(11) A man demanded money from a woman who was near a cash register.

(12) Money from the cash register was given to the man wearing a hat.

(13) The man argued with the woman.

(14) The woman opened the cash register.

(15) Someone scooped up the contents of the cash register.

(16) The man got the money he had demanded.

(17) The man had a car waiting for him.

(18) A man wearing a hat sped away with the money.

(19) The owner notified the police promptly.

(20) The man left his hat behind.

(21) The police were summoned.

(22) The police officer took the hat as evidence.

(23) A policeman discussed the matter, took the hat, and drove off.

(24) No customer was involved in the story.

(25) The man had remained calm throughout the whole incident.

Answers

(1) Four people were involved in the story.

? It could be four (owner, man, woman, police officer) or three (the owner and the woman being the same person).

(2) Only one woman was involved in the story.

? Either or both the owner and the police officer could be women.

(3) Three women were involved in the story.

? See above answers.

(4) The robbery took place at the cash register.

? It might have, but then again there might have been no robbery at all. The man may have had legitimate reasons for demanding money (e.g., he was the son of the woman and was late for a date).

(5) The incident did not take place at the end of the business day.

? It might have been the beginning of a business day, since the owner was unlocking the front door; but the restaurant may open at the end of someone else's "business day," or the unlocking of the door might have had nothing to do with the time of day.

(6) The owner of the restaurant was present during the incident.

? Perhaps, but the owner might have been unlocking the door of the store across the street from the site of the incident. The unlocking of the door and the appearance of the man are only contemporaneous ("when").

(7) The owner unlocked the front door from the inside.

? Even if it were the beginning of a business day at a restaurant, the owner could be opening the door from the outside (having just arrived) or from the outside (having let himself or herself in by another door).

(8) The man who owned the restaurant unlocked the front door.

? Perhaps, but the owner could have been a woman.

(9) The owner unlocked the front door of the restaurant.

? Perhaps, but the owner may have opened the door to some building other than the restaurant.

(10) A man wearing a hat entered by the door that the owner had just unlocked.

? Perhaps, but the man just "appeared" and could have done so from some other entrance or could have been there before the unlocking.

(11) A man demanded money from a woman who was near a cash register.

True.

(12) Money from the cash register was given to the man wearing a hat.

? Perhaps, but the cash register may have had "contents" other than money, and the money that he "sped away with" may have nothing to do with the "contents" of the cash register.

(13) The man argued with the woman.

? Perhaps, but his "demanding" does not constitute an argument, and the "words exchanged" may have been with the owner of the restaurant or some unidentified person.

(14) The woman opened the cash register.

? Perhaps, but the cash register could have been opened by anyone else present.

(15) Someone scooped up the contents of the cash register.

True.

(16) The man got the money he had demanded.

True.

(17) The man had a car waiting for him.

? He might have, but he might have "sped away" on a motorcycle just as easily.

(18) A man wearing a hat sped away with the money.

? Although it looks like a man without a hat did the speeding away, it is possible that he had another hat in the car, or he might have had a behatted accomplice in the car.

(19) The owner notified the police promptly.

? Perhaps, but we do not know precisely who telephoned the police.

(20) The man left his hat behind.

True.

(21) The police were summoned.

? "The police were summoned" implies that they were summoned in their roles as police. The "member of the police force" who was "telephoned" in this case might well have been a friend of the family, asked over for personal reasons. E.g.: The man with the hat is the son of a restauranteur. He appears at the restaurant in full formal dress, on his way to his best friend's wedding, to show off his finery and hit up his mother for a few bucks. She chides him for being late and for not tying his tie correctly. They exchange words about it, and he feels harrassed and becomes annoyed, so much so that when she finally gives him money from the cash register, he runs out without his top hat. A cousin of theirs, who is to attend the same wedding and happens to be a member of the police force, is phoned. Luckily he has not yet left for the wedding, and he agrees to stop by the restaurant, listen to a few maternal complaints, and transport the hat to the wedding.

(22) The police officer took the hat as evidence.

? If a robbery had occurred, perhaps; if it was the wedding suggested in #21, no.

(23) A policeman discussed the matter, took the hat, and drove off.

? Perhaps, but nothing tells us it was not a policewoman instead.

(24) No customer was involved in the story.

? Since the incident might have involved only an owner, a cashier, a robber, and a police officer, the statement could be true. On the other hand, since the incident might have happened in a Dry Cleaner's shop, the restaurant owner could have been a customer, making the statement false. Even if the locale was the restaurant of the owner, the woman who was standing at the cash register might have been a customer waiting to pay her bill.

(25) The man had remained calm throughout the whole incident.

False

Here is another, without the answers.

EXERCISE

Read the following narrative carefully, accepting all of it as true. Then label each of the 20 statements that follow as either "True," "False," or "?". "True" means that the statement can be absolutely verified by the information given in the narrative. "False" means that the statement can be absolutely disproved by the information given in the narrative. "?" means that the statement could be either true or false, given the information in the narrative.

For each answer of "?", demonstrate how the statement might be true and might be false, given the information in the narrative.

Narrative

"I don't care if you're my brother, I'm going to kill you!" the man in the blue suit shouted at someone in the house as he ran out, slamming the door. Ten minutes later he returned, clasping a brown paper bag. He banged on the door yelling, "Let me in!". The door opened and he entered. Loud noises of shouting were heard from within the house. A noise like a gun shot rang out. The police arrived soon after with an ambulance. Minutes later they carried out a man in a blue suit on a stretcher. He was groaning.

Statements

(1) A man and his brother were involved in the incident.

(2) The man in the blue suit intended to kill his brother.

(3) No one was in the house when the man in the blue suit returned.

(4) The man in the blue suit was having an argument with the person in the house.

(5) The man in the blue suit left the house to get something in a paper bag.

(6) The man in the blue suit was in a hurry as he left the house the first time.

(7) The man in the blue suit returned to the house with a gun in a paper bag.

(8) The man in the blue suit left the house to summon the police.

(9) The police came because a noise like a shot rang out.

(10) Someone in the house opened the door when the man in the blue suit yelled "Let me in!".

(11) Loud shouting could be heard from those inside the house.

(12) A shot rang out.

(13) The police were notified about the incident.

(14) The man who had shouted "I'm going to kill you" was carried away on a stretcher.

(15) The man on the stretcher was groaning.

(16) The man on the stretcher was in pain.

(17) The man on the stretcher sounded like he was in pain.

(18) The man in the blue suit intended to scare or to harm the person in the house.

(19) Something illegal happened in the house.

(20) We know for certain that the man in the blue suit and the person in the house were not meeting for the first time.

C.   DETERMINING FACTS

Two automobiles collide at an intersection, causing severe damage to both. One driver escapes injury, but the other driver and his passenger suffer some broken bones and bruises. One witness saw it all. Everything happened in a few seconds. How does one go about determining "the facts"?

Only these four people (the two drivers, the passenger, and the witness) were present at the time of the collision. The whole thing happened so quickly that everyone was taken by surprise. Each may be telling the "truth" as he or she perceived it, but each has a different emotional perspective on the accident, each notices detail differently, and each saw it literally from a different angle. Each, therefore, gives a different version of "the accident." What then is "the accident"?

If the case comes to court, the finder of fact, be it judge or jury, will eventually make a decision as to what happened, and for all legal purposes that version of "the facts" becomes "the accident." The establishing of the likelihood of "the facts" therefore becomes the lawyer's central task in such a case. Clarence Darrow used to boast, "If you let me state the facts, I'll let you argue the Law."

A lawyer must be able to sift all the information available in a given situation, separating the incontrovertible from the highly probable from the possible from the unlikely. He or she must have an understanding of what is crucial, what is significant, and what is irrelevant. All arguments made, agreements fashioned, and advice given depends directly on the accuracy, completeness, and logical organization made of the basic information. Where "fact" is not apparent, probability will have to be argued, and it is crucial for a lawyer to be able to recognize the difference between the two.

There is no easy and quick way to become expert in separating the meaningful from the meaningless, the probably true from the possibly false, the logical conclusion from the need-prompted inference. It takes much experience, much trial and error, to become adept at it. You can steadily improve your defenses against illogicality, inference, and mistaken "fact" by following these few guide-lines when considering and organizing the material happenings upon which your problem is based:

(1) Define the situation before you; that is, state as clearly as possible everything that is necessary to the situation while excluding everything extraneous to it.

(2) Limit ambiguity wherever possible.

(3) Leave nothing to the inference of others that you can articulate explicitly yourself.

(4) Separate the accepted facts from the matters that need to be argued.

At this point you will be close to understanding the shape of the situation before you, and you will be ready to start forming an argument.

EXERCISE

Hypothetical:

Two automobiles have collided at an intersection, causing severe damage to both. Mr. D., driver of car D, escaped unharmed. Mr. P. and Mrs. P., driver and passenger of car P, suffered some broken bones and bruises. Witness W., a pedestrian, saw the accident while waiting to cross the intersection. Both drivers feel they were not at fault, and the case will have to be settled in court.

Your law firm represents Mr. and Mrs. P. One of your colleagues has interviewed Mr. P., Mrs. P., Mr. D., and the witness, W. She gives you the following four transcripts of those interviews and asks you to sift through the material and report to her on the following questions:

(1) What "facts" can we rely on?

(2) What other details can we consider highly probable and likely to be viewed by the court from our perspective, assuming a good argument by us?

(3) What are the "facts" against us?

(4) What other details may be strongly argued against us?

(5) What details or issues are "up for grabs," as it were, and how can we best work on them?

(6) What extra information do we need, and how can we get it?

She also wants you to arrange what we do feel sure about at the moment into a Statement of Fact.

Task:

Answer your colleague's six questions and prepare the Statement of Fact insofar as you are able, given the present information.

Transcript of Interview Between Lawyer L and Mr. P.

L: What is your name?

Mr. P.:   Joe P.

L: What is your address?

Mr. P.:   563 North Conway Boulevard, Fair City.

L: Were you involved in an automobile accident with Mr. D.?

Mr. P.:   Yes.

L: When was that?

Mr. P.:   December 23 of last year. I remember because it was two days before the Christmas party my mother-in-law always throws. We were going shopping for some last minute presents.

L: When was the accident, what time of day?

Mr. P.:   About 3:30 in the afternoon.

L: Where did it happen?

Mr. P.:   It was at the intersection of Riverside and Bakersville. We were heading in town along Riverside. He was coming from the other direction.

L: You were going east on Riverside and he was going west?

Mr. P.:   That's right.

L: Who was involved in the accident?

Mr. P.:   Well, there was only me and my wife in our car, and only him in the other car. Nobody else was involved.

L: By "him," you mean Mr. D.?

Mr. P.:   Uh huh. Yes.

L: What kind of car were you driving?

Mr. P.:   It was our family car, the station wagon. 1979 Dodge. Blue.

L: What kind of car was Mr. D. driving?

Mr. P.:   It was a cream-colored sports car, one of those expensive models. Something foreign. I can't tell one from another. Just the car for a rich kid like him. He never even looked where he was going.

L: Would you please describe the accident as you saw it happen?

Mr. P.:   Well, we were going in town, like I told you, for some Christmas shopping. We had to get a present for my mother-in-law. We'd looked for one two times already, but my wife is kind of particular about what we get her mother, and we hadn't found anything that would be exactly the right thing. So we were going along, O, I'd say at 25, maybe 30 miles an hour, and we reached the intersection of Riverside and Bakersville Road, you know, where the bridge goes off to the right over the river. We started into the intersection when the light was green but it turned yellow just after we got into it; but since we were already in it I naturally kept going, you know, like the State's book of driving rules tells you to do. Well, this kid comes barreling through in his sports car. I'd say he was doing about 45. He must have gone through a yellow light from the start, because I was in the intersection way before him and the light turned yellow while I was there but before he showed up. Well, I swerved to try to avoid him, but he was cutting in front of me to try to take the turn up onto the bridge. So as I swerved to the right, he kept going in that direction, too. We must have hit about two-thirds of the way through the intersection—from my side, that is—and we skidded off towards the gutter. It was one hell of a crash.—O I'm sorry, I forgot you were taperecording this. Well, it was a real big bash, so to speak, and both cars got pretty badly smashed up.

L: Did you brake when you saw him?

Mr. P.:   Yeah, I hit the brakes the minute I saw him.

L: Are you sure you didn't try to swerve first, before applying the brakes?

Mr. P.:   Yeah. No. I mean, I hit the brakes and swerved at the same time.

L: Would you describe the condition of the cars after the accident?

Mr. P.:   They were both pretty bad, like I said before. We couldn't drive either one away. They both had to be towed. The police came right away and asked a lot of questions.

L: How much damage was there to your car, in dollars?

Mr. P.:   It totalled up to $3,500, almost.

L: Do you know how much damage there was to his car?

Mr. P.:   No, but it didn't look as bad as mine.

L: Were there any injuries to any of you?

Mr. P.:   I broke two bones in my hand, my right hand, and dislocated an elbow. I was wearing my seat belt, but I was holding the wheel kind of funny, and the impact must have snapped something. My wife, well she wasn't wearing her seat belt. I can never get her to wear the danged thing. She says she never wore them before, so she sees no reason to wear them now. Funny thing is, I came out of the accident worse than she did. She banged her head into the windshield and smashed the thing pretty good. The windshield, I mean. Her head came out O.K., the doctors said, but I think she was really lucky. She's had some headaches since, but I don't think they have anything to do with her hitting the windshield like that, because they didn't start until about a week afterwards.

L: Is that all?

Mr. P.: I think so.

L: What about Mr. D.? Was he injured?

Mr. P.: Nah. Isn't that just the way? The guy causes an accident, wrecks my hand, nearly kills my wife, and walks away without a scratch.

L.: So you would say the accident was his fault?

Mr. P.: Absolutely. I didn't do anything wrong, and he went through the yellow light and cut in front of me.

L.: Thank you very much for your co-operation.

Transcript of Interview Between Lawyer L and Mrs. P.

L: What is your name, please?

Mrs. P.: Jenny P.

L: What is your address?

Mrs. P.: 563 North Conway Boulevard, Fair City.

L: Were you involved in an automobile accident with Mr. D.?

Mrs. P.: No, my husband was. I was just in the car.

L: When was that?

Mrs. P.: December 22 of last year. It was two days before my mother's annual Christmas party, but she was throwing it on Christmas Eve last year because my sister couldn't stay through Christmas day. We were going shopping for her present and we only had two days left. That's how I remember it.

L: At what time of day was the accident?

Mrs. P.: It was late afternoon. I remember being so mad at my husband because he was dragging his feet about going into town and shopping on a day off. It must have been past 4:00 by the time we got going, so I would say we got to the place where the accident happened about 4:15.

L: Where did the accident happen?

Mrs. P.:   It was on Riverside at that big street that goes off to the left towards Bakersville. I don't know exactly what the name of that street is. It was the one where the bridge goes off to the right.

L: Which direction were the two cars going in?

Mrs. P.:   You mean east or west or that kind of thing? I've never gotten used to those things. We didn't have them where I grew up. We were going in-town on Riverside and he was coming out of town on Riverside and decided to take a left turn onto the bridge—through us.

L: Who was in the two cars that were involved?

Mrs. P.:   My husband and I were in our car, and he was in his car. No one else.

L: By "he," you mean Mr. D.?

Mrs. P.:   Yes.

L: What was the make and year of your car.

Mrs. P.:   It was the station wagon, a Dodge, blue. 1978, I think.

L: What kind of car was Mr. D. driving?

Mrs. P.:   It was one of those little sports cars, beige. I don't exactly know what kind.

L: Would you please describe the accident as you saw it happen?

Mrs. P.:   Well, like I said before, we were going shopping, and it was late, and we were arguing about what we should get Mother. We argue about how much to spend on Mother every year, but it always comes out alright. We never guess the right thing, and she always takes it back and exchanges it for something else, so I like to give her something just a little bit more expensive each year, so she'll at least think we keep up with inflation when we buy her a gift. I'm afraid I was a bit too hard on him this year, and I think that's why he was going so fast.

L: Excuse me. How fast would you say he was going?

Mrs. P.:   O, I couldn't say for sure. You know how you only get an approximate feel for those sorts of things when you're in the passenger's seat.

L: Would you say he was going over the speed limit? Over thirty miles an hour?

Mrs. P.:   I couldn't say. It just seemed fast, but maybe I shouldn't say that.

L: Well, go on with your description.

Mrs. P.:   Well, we got to that intersection and halfway through the intersection this young man in the sports car cut in front of us and we hit him. I mean, he hit us, too. It was almost head-on. That was it.

L: Did you notice what color the light was when you entered the intersection?

Mrs. P.:   No. You know you never look at those things when you're not driving yourself. It all happened so fast, and I remember I was saying something about the store going to be closed and then wham! We never made it to the store.

L: Did your husband try to swerve when he saw the other car?

Mrs. P.:   We swerved, all right. I think he was trying to avoid him. The brakes were screeching and everything. I'd never been in an accident before. You just say to yourself, real slowly, "We are going to smash into that car in front of us,", and wham!, you do.

L: Can you describe the actions of the other car?

Mrs. P.:   I wasn't watching him. He was just there all of a sudden. I think he was travelling pretty fast, though, although it's hard to say.

L: Can you describe the condition of the cars after the smash?

Mrs. P.:   They both had to be towed away. Ours took a whole lot of repair work, over $3,000.

L: Do you know how much damage there was to his car?

Mrs. P.:   No. It looked pretty bad, too. Maybe not quite so bad as ours, though.

L: Was anyone injured?

Mrs. P.:   O yes. I smashed my head on the windshield, and I've had the worst headaches ever since. But the doctor said I didn't break anything and that I was really lucky. I think I'd better start wearing seat belts, now that I think about it. I just hate the things, but I bet I wouldn't have these headaches if I had been wearing a seat belt. My husband broke a couple of bones in his hand and did something to his elbow, but he's O.K. now. It was really annoying to him at the time, though. I think he was really in quite a bit of pain.

L: Is that all?

Mrs. P.:   As far as I can remember.

L: What about Mr. D.? Was he injured?

Mrs. P.:   No. He seemed O.K. I don't even know if he went to the hospital or not.

L: Who was at fault in the accident, in your opinion?

Mrs. P.:   Well, I thought about it for a long time, and I think he was, Mr. D., that is. He shouldn't have turned right in front of us—I mean turned just in front of us—and he was going pretty fast, at least as fast as we were. I think it was his fault.

L: Thank you very much for you co-operation.

Transcript of Interview Between Lawyer L and Mr. D.

L: What is your name, please?

Mr. D.:   Thornton D.

L: Where do you live?

Mr. D.:   At The Brambles, Fairtown.

L: Were you involved in an accident with Mr. and Mrs. P.?

Mr. D.:   Yes.

L: When was that?

Mr. D.:   December 22, 3:35 P.M.

L: How are you so sure of the time?

Mr. D.: My car's clock was broken by the impact. It stopped at 3:35 P.M.

L: Was your car's clock never fast nor slow before the accident?

Mr. D.: Never.

L: Where did it happen?

Mr. D.: At the intersection of Riverside and Bakersville Road.

L: Which directions were the two cars coming from?

Mr. D.: I was driving west on Riverside and taking a left turn onto the bridge. They were driving east on Riverside.

L: Was anyone involved in the accident besides yourself and Mr. and Mrs. P.?

Mr. D.: No.

L: What kind of car were you driving?

Mr. D.: A 1979 white Lambretta DXL.

L: What kind of car was Mr. P. driving?

Mr. D.: A 1978 blue Dodge station wagon, the Vacationeer model.

L: Would you please describe the accident as you saw it happen?

Mr. D.: I was proceeding west on Riverside at precisely 30 miles per hour.

L: Excuse me, how are you sure it was precisely 30?

Mr. D.: I always drive precisely thirty in thirty-mile-an-hour zones. I approached the intersection, reduced my speed, and signalled for a left turn. The light was green, and the approaching traffic seemed far enough in the distance to negotiate the turn safely. While I was making the turn, Mr. P.'s car sped into the intersection, going through a yellow light, and hit me. Mr. P. was travelling well over 40 miles an hour, perhaps 47 or 48.

L: Did you try to avoid the collision in any way?

Mr. D.: When I saw he was not going to stop I floored the accelerator, hoping I could at least get out of his way,

but he swerved in the direction I was turning and hit
me.

L: Would you describe the condition of the cars after the
         accident?

Mr. D.: Both cars were immobilized and had to be towed away.
         I could not estimate how much his repairs might have
         been, but mine totalled $4,375.

L: Were there any injuries to any of you?

Mr. D.: His wife looked like she had hit her head rather severe-
         ly against the windshield, which was broken. I don't
         know what happened, but I can imagine she might have
         suffered a minor concussion. He looked unharmed, al-
         though he was quite hysterical. I was unharmed.

L: Who would you say was at fault in this accident?

Mr. D.: The accident was clearly his fault. He was speeding,
         and he went through a yellow light. I was driving at
         the speed limit, at least until I tried to avoid him, and
         had gone through a green light.

L: Thank you very much for your co-operation.

Transcript of Interview Between Lawyer L and Witness W

L: What is your name, please?

W: W.

L: What is your address?

W: Don't have one right now.

L: Where or how can we reach you?

W: Through my friend, like you did this time.

L: Did you witness an automobile accident in December of
         last year?

W: Yes.

L: Where and when was it?

W: It was at the corner of Riverside and the bridge some-
         time just before Christmas, in the afternoon.

L: Do you remember the exact time?

W: No.

L: What direction were the cars going before they hit?

W: The white one was going to the right and the blue one was going to the left. Then the white one tried to turn up onto the bridge, but he didn't make it. That's when they smashed.

L: Do you know who was involved in this accident?

W: I never saw them before. There was a young guy in the white car and a man and a woman in the blue one.

L: Would you please describe the accident just as you saw it happen?

W: I just did. Is there something else you want extra?

L: Were either of the cars going particularly fast?

W: Hard to say. I think the blue car was going real fast all the time. The white one was going real fast, and then he braked as if he wasn't going to try the turn, and then he took off for the bridge. They were both going pretty fast when they hit. It was a real smash-up. Glass all over the place.

L: Could you tell anything about what color the traffic lights were?

W: The one in front of me was red, all the time.

L: But you don't know about the ones they were looking at?

W: Nah, but from the way that guy in the white car hit the brakes, I'd say that the light must have just turned yellow on him, but he decided to take the chance anyway.

L: Which car was in the intersection first?

W: Tough to say, it all happened so quick. If I had to, I'd put my money on the blue one. I think he was in there first. It was close, though, so I wouldn't give no odds.

L: Would you describe the condition of the cars after the accident?

W: Yeah, that's easy. They was wrecked. The tow truck musta made a buck out of that one, towing both of them away. The mechanic probably cashed in on it, too.

L: Did you notice if anyone was injured?

W: Yeah, the guy in the blue car was yelling like crazy and holding his arm, so I think he must have busted it up pretty good. The lady in the blue car looked kinda out of it, and she was holding her head and bawling a little. The guy in the white car didn't seem hurt, and he didn't seem to care too much about the other guys.

L: Whose fault would you say the accident was?

W: Like I said before, I'd bet the guy in the blue car was in the right if I had to bet, but it was a close one, that's for sure.

L: Thank you very much for your co-operation.

Chapter VII

TRANSLATION

This chapter concentrates further on critical reading abilities. In the previous Chapter we dealt mostly with the mode of Narration; here we switch to the mode of Exposition. We will analyze four articles from major city newspapers, asking:

(1) What does the article promise to tell us?
(2) What does the article actually tell us?
(3) What does the article fail to tell us?

This process will afford you an opportunity to use your knowledge of the nature of definitions, inferences, and facts discussed in previous chapters. Once you have discovered the ways in which the articles fail to live up to their promises, you will then be prepared to "translate" them into the articles they should have been, that is, to rewrite them as they should have been written in the first place, to articulate exactly what it was they were trying to say.

Close and critical reading takes both time and intellectual energy, but we are usually well paid for the effort with clearer understanding. It is difficult at first to separate the picayune criticisms from the significant ones, but that ability will develop over time. Also, it is easier to perceive the flaws in the material included than to discover what has been omitted. This ability too develops over time.

We are often more impressed by newspaper articles than we should be. We allow ourselves to be swayed by the impressive but illusive authority of print. Newspaper articles are often shoddily written, perhaps because of the pressures of quick publication, which often deny journalists the time necessary for reflection and revision, and which force editors to concern themselves more with time and space than with style and accuracy. As a result, some newspapers make fine textbooks for the student of critical reading, providing a continual source of intense but flawed prose.

163

You should read quickly your first time through these articles, as the journalists who wrote them would expect you to do. Then take a few minutes to paraphrase in writing the main points of the article, so that when you have finished the analyses and exercises you will be able to see if you overestimated or underestimated the depth of the article on first reading. You may well find a great difference between what you thought you had read and what you later discovered actually to be there.

The kind of error detection we are engaged in here parallels the critical reading process a lawyer uses when reading legal documents. You should allow the writers no inferences, no undue assumptions about your previous knowledge, no good will on your part to piece together what they have left fractured. You may even find yourself well amused by this process.

Article # 1

Read the article and paraphrase in a few sentences what you perceive its subject and main points to be. Then consider closely the thirty-three questions which follow it. Responses to the questions follow, but you would do well to try to formulate your own before reading on.

COUNCIL SEES
NEED TO
ASSESS ROLE

Law Fulfillment
"Seldom Done"

(1) The State Manpower Planning Services Council decided Tuesday it would undertake a fundamental reassessment of its role in state government.

(2) Meeting at the State Board of Education Building, 470 East Fifth Street, council members agreed that historically they have not effectively achieved their primary function as defined by state law.

(3) The law says the council will "formulate goals, objectives and policies to govern the development and administration of manpower programs in the state."

(4) But, as he traced the evolution of the council since 1967, Carl L. Burtonson, state planning coordinator and council executive director, pointed out that has seldom been done.

Special Task Force

(5) At the urging of Philip Harmado, council chairman, the council voted unanimously to establish a special task force to work with the council staff to define the precise role of the panel.

(6) Mr. Harmado said he will meet with the council's executive committee to appoint the task force.

(7) "We are getting to be a funny looking elephant," Mr. Harmado told the council. "We have a very blurred self-image of what we are doing."

(8) A major part of the problem is that legislative action since the council was established has swollen the panel to 36 members, a number too large to be effective, Mr. Burtonson said.

Membership Defined

(9) Legislation in 1969 specifically defined which state agencies—some of which no longer exist or are drastically altered—would be represented on the council, Mr. Burtonson explained.

(10) Through its own by-laws, the council elected to add a number of positions on the council, Mr. Burtonson said, and then federal legislation added still more.

(11) The Comprehensive Employment and Training Act (CETA) made it necessary for the governor to expand the council through executive order, Mr. Burtonson added.

Planning Function

(12) Dr. Van Chambers, council member representing the adult vocational and rehabilitation services of the State Board of Education, reminded his colleagues that many times the council has gotten involved in the actual operation of programs instead of the more important function of planning.

(13) The role of actually delivering services has been effectively taken over by local manpower councils, Mr. Burtonson declared, and it is time the council assumed its proper role of setting goals, establishing priorities and drafting policies.

(14) Mr. Burtonson also urged the council to maintain a broad base and establish a structure for dealing with the young, the old, women, energy and growth demands of the future.

Reassess Role

(15) Many of the current problems, in terms of size and structure, can only be resolved by legislative action, Mr. Harmado observed. He recommended that the council's timetable for reassessment of its role, structure and goals be keyed to next year's legislative session.

Questions for Article # 1

(1) What do you know from the title, "Council Sees Need to Assess Role"?

(2) What does this title lead you to expect from the article?

(3) What does the subtitle "Law Fulfillment Seldom Done" mean?

(4) Why does the writer inform us of the location of the meeting (¶ 2)?

(5) What does "historically" mean in ¶ 2?

(6) What is meant by "have not effectively achieved their primary function" (¶ 2)? What is weak, awkward, or ambiguous about this phrase?

(7) Explain their "primary function as defined by state law," given only the information in the article (¶ 2).

(8) To what does "that" refer (¶ 2)?

(9) What has the council done since 1967, according to this article?

(10) What is the distinction between the jobs of Mr. Burtonson and Mr. Harmado?

(11) From where will the members of the "special task force" be chosen (¶ 5)?

(12) Distinguish between "council," "special task force," "council staff," and "panel" (¶ 5).

(13) What does Mr. Harmado mean by "We are getting to be a funny looking elephant" (¶ 7)?

(14) Analyze Mr. Harmado's comment, "We have a very blurred self-image of what we are doing" (¶ 7).

(15) What is the relationship between the idea(s) in the eighth paragraph and those in the previous seven paragraphs?

(16) What does the sub-heading "Membership Defined" promise? Does the article fulfill that promise?

(17) One reason the council is so large, the article suggests, is that the legislature "defined" which agencies should be represented; but some of those agencies "no longer exist" or have been "drastically altered" (¶ 9). Analyze this logic.

(18) Is the expansion referred to in the eleventh paragraph in addition to or the same as that mentioned in the tenth paragraph?

(19) Of what importance is it, according to what you know from the article, who is responsible for the large size of the council?

(20) According to the article, why does the council's large size prevent it from acting effectively?

(21) What effect does the size of the council have on its defining its rule under the statute that created it?

(22) What might the sub-heading "Planning Function" suggest?

(23) Dr. Chambers seems to regret the council's involvement in "the actual operation of programs instead of the more important function of planning" (¶ 12). Analyze this statement and his attitude.

(24) Is it good or bad that the local councils have taken over "the role of actually delivering services" (¶ 12)? Were they supposed to have done this?

(25) Distinguish between "goals," "priorities," and "policies" (¶ 13).

(26) What does Mr. Burtonson mean by urging the council "to maintain a broad base" (¶ 14)?

(27) According to the article, is there already a structure for dealing with areas other than "the young, the old, women," etc. (¶ 14)?

(28) What does the sub-heading "Reassess Role" promise? What is actually delivered?

(29) Given the information in the final paragraph, and the problems raised by the council's representatives in the rest of the article, what role are we to expect the council to fulfill until "next year's legislative session" convenes (¶ 15)?

(30) Given only the information in this article, define the actual scope of this council's power and interests. With whom does it deal, and how?

(31) Now what seems to you to be the subject of this article? (Compare with your response to Question 2 above.)

(32) What is "manpower," and what therefore would any "Manpower Planning Services Council" be expected to do?

(33) If you were hired as a consultant to this council, what would you advise that they ask "next year's legislature to do?

Responses to Questions for Article #1

The Council, apparently, is concerned about something.

(1) We assumed that it has not previously assessed this role, for then the title would have read "Reassess Role." We do not know whose role the are assessing or why.

(2) We expect to find out what Council, whose role, and why it needs assessment (all of which happen); but we also might expect to understand the nature of the "role," which never quite comes clear.

(3) It might suggest that the "role" is one of "law fulfillment," that the person or agency being investigated has some policing powers. It is difficult to understand what the word "law" means in its adjectival position here. How exactly does one "do" a "law fulfillment"?

(4) While it is conceivable that the location of the meeting might have some significance for one who knows a great deal about this city's government, its inclusion here is probably *pro forma*, one of the journalistic questions that

"must" be answered (the "where" of "who, what, when, where, why, and how").

(5) It sounds like "history" has defined the role of a "Manpower Planning Services Council," or that this particular Council has been around for so long that it merits "historical" standing (which seems to be contradicted by the dates given in the fourth paragraph).

(6) These words may sound sophisticated, but they have been misapplied when used in this combination. One cannot "achieve" a "function"; nor can one "achieve" anything ineffectively. The phrase also implies that their secondary functions have enjoyed a better fate.

(7) This proves most difficult to do. Even if the quoted law in the third paragraph were specific enough to have a functional meaning, we could not choose one of the three tasks as "primary." To call all three "primary" would be to impoverish the word. The reporter, it seems, fails to understand what their "primary function" is because they have failed to understand it. If they are confused, and the reporter is confused, how are we to be expected to make sense out of it? The major weakness of the article is that it continually gives the impression that everyone does understand the situation, and that the article is merely bringing us up to date on it.

(8) I imagine "that" was to have referred to the "primary function" supposedly defined in the third paragraph. However, syntactically "that" refers to "tracing the evolution of the council since 1967," which makes the sentence at best silly, at the worst, nonsensical.

(9) It has "swollen" (¶ 8) and "gotten involved in the actual operation of programs," both of which it apparently should not have done. Its other activities, if indeed there were any, are hidden from us.

(10) Here we see the effects of bureaucratic nomenclature. "State planning coordinator," "council executive director," and "council chairman" seem on the one hand to be indistinguishable until further defined, or on the other hand to be three people, or perhaps one, but hardly two.

(11) We do not know, and yet it seems of at least as much import as anything else in the article.

(12) The second body referred to is not yet in existence; the other three, for all one can tell, are indistinguishable. It is possible, however, that "council" refers to the voting members of the agency, "council staff" to those others who do the actual day-to-day work of the agency, and "panel" to a selected few of the "council" chosen to look into this particular matter. The writer seems to imply such distinctions by using three different terms, but the rest of the writing is inaccurate enough to make us suspect that he might only have been searching for synonyms so that he would not repeat himself.

(13) Only Mr. Harmado knows for sure.

(14) Once again words collide meaninglessly. Unless the speaker is engaged in comparing various blurs, there can be no distinction between "blurred" and "very blurred." Moreover, a single "image" cannot simultaneously represent both the "self" and "what we are doing," so it is impossible to have a "self-image of what we are doing." (It reaches the point of the ridiculous when funny looking elephants have very blurred self-images of what they are doing.)

(15) The eighth paragraph comes as complete surprise. Nothing in the first seven paragraphs prepares us for this discussion of size.

(16) The sub-heading suggests that we will learn precisely who makes up the membership of the Council, but instead we learn only how and when the Council grew in size.

(17) When an agency is dissolved, its members, by definition, no longer exist. This process, if it affects the Manpower Council at all, should decrease the size of the Council, not augment it as the article implies. Perhaps the writer is broaching yet another troubled subject, the nature of the membership, but the middle of a sentence that has introduced a new topic is no place for the introduction of yet a newer one.

(18) On the one hand, CETA is indeed "federal legislation" which "added still more" to the size of the Council, thus making

¶ 11 seem to be a further explanation of ¶ 10. On the other hand, the fact that the information about CETA appears in a paragraph of its own (underscored by the use of the verb "added") indicates that ¶ 11 gives us information that must be considered distinct from that of ¶ 10.

(19) The best that can be done with this is none too good. It seems that on the one hand the Council is at fault for not understanding what it should be doing; but on the other hand it is prevented from understanding because it is too big, which is the fault of numerous other people and agencies. Thus the Council is to be blamed but not to be blamed. Furthermore, we are not informed why fewer people (that is, a smaller Council) could better pierce this veil of ignorance.

(20) The article is silent on this subject.

(21) The article is silent on this subject as well.

(22) It might suggest that the Council is planning a large party, perhaps a fund-raising benefit or an anniversary party. Alternatively it might suggest that "planning" is the "primary function" of the Council.

(23) Dr. Chambers suggests that the planning of programs is somehow "more important" than the actualizing of them, a strange concept. In order to understand why he should make such a statement, we have to infer a good deal. Perhaps he meant that planning is more important to the functioning of the Council than is the actual operation; perhaps by "actual operation" he refers to the petty details of operating the programs, any one of which is less "important" than the broader planning function; or perhaps as a representative of the adult vocational and rehabilitation services of the Board of Education, which might have control of the "actual operation" of certain programs, he is annoyed at the Council's usurpation of his agency's powers. In any event, we have to work much too hard to figure the situation out, when we have a journalist who is supposed to have done it for us.

(24) The article does not clarify either of these concerns.

(25) As in Question #10 above, these abstract terms cry out for definition each time they are used in a new context. In a vacuum, as they are presented to us here, they can have little if any meaning.

(26) He suggests by the word "maintain" that the Council already has a "broad base" but is in danger of losing it unless it expands operations by establishing a "structure" for other activities. It is not clear exactly what a "broad base" might be.

(27) Mr. Burtonson has implied that such structures exist, but the article in general seems to complain that the Council has no structure(s) and must reassess its role as a result. The ambiguities and the obscurities increase.

(28) It promises the answer to the issue raised by the initial title and most of the inquiries along the way; a way for the Council to reassess its role and redefine itself. It delivers only the hope that "next year's legislative session" might do something about it.

(29) We can expect the Council to cease doing what it should not (involving itself in the actual operation of programs), but we cannot expect it to do anything else because it does not understand what it is supposed to be doing. In short, we can expect the Council to sit on its hands, waiting for next year's legislature to solve the problem.

(30) By this time this question should raise intense feelings of frustration and annoyance.

(31) The true subject of the article seems to be how the Council has avoided facing up to the supposed subject of the article, the reassessment and redefinition of its purposes.

(32) These questions have not been approached by the article.

(33) If you can answer this question, you are capable of rewriting this article the way it should have appeared in the first place.

EXERCISE

In expending a good deal of effort in trying to understand what this article actually says and what it should have said, you have experienced how insidious an aggregation of little loose ends of logic can prove in expository prose. They can multiply, as they did here, until almost all meaning fades away in a mist of well intended verbiage.

Rewrite this article, manufacturing whatever knowledge you need to make sense of the situation. Choose a title that makes a specific promise to the reader, and then be sure to keep it. You may create quotes for the representatives of the Council, invent tasks they should have done or ought to be doing; in short, do anything necessary to complete the task that this journalist started.

Here are two more articles with appended questions. Perform the same functions on them that you did for the first article.

Article #2

October 26

POLICE ISSUE CON ARTISTS WARNING

(1) Con artists, whose potential victims are elderly widows, Thursday prompted city police detectives to issue a warning against shady financial dealings with two women.

(2) Det. Ford Carsling said eight cases of "pigeon dropping" have been reported this summer, with two occurring Wednesday.

(3) Both incidents were identical and each involved the attempted duping of 70-year-old widows.

(4) According to Det. Carsling, one of the women "happens" along while the older women work outside in their yards.

Small Talk

(5) Usually, small talk concerning where to rent an apartment preceded another woman coming by with a purse full of cash.

(6) The women, both widows who told the suspects that they had money resulting from the recent losses of their husbands, were then told that one suspect was employed by an attorney and that she would talk to him about what to do with the found loot.

Asked for Savings

(7) It was then the elderly widows were asked for their savings as security.

(8) Neither of the women fell for their ploy but Det. Carsling said the game has been successful many times before.

(9) In June, an elderly woman was bilked out of her life's savings—over $17,000—by three women who employed similar means to gain her confidence. That money was never recovered.

(10) Det. Carsling said bank tellers and managers should also be suspicious when older people want to withdraw their savings, particularly if they want it in cash.

Questions for Article #2

This delightfully (but unintentionally) zany article resembles a Peter Sellers movie in which he plays all the leading roles himself. You need a scorecard to keep the players straight, who is taking, who is being taken, who is being warned against whom, etc.

(1) The title offers multiple possibilities for interpretation. What are they?

(2) According to the strange grammar in ¶ 1, who warned whom about what, and why?

(3) On the basis of your knowledge gained from the first two paragraphs only, what do you take "pigeon dropping" to mean?

(4) How many cases of "pigeon dropping" are referred to in ¶ 2? Note that the article was written on October 26.)

(5) What is wrong with the first four words of ¶ 3?

(6) Grammatically, to whom must the "women" in ¶ 4 refer? Why is this confusing?

(7) Are the "older women" of ¶ 4 part of the plot, "planted," as it were, in their yards? Or are they the intended victims?

(8) What is wrong with the concept of small talk preceding another woman? (¶ 5)

(9) To whom do the following terms refer in ¶ 6: "the women," "widows," "the suspects," "they," "their," and "she"?

(10) What is the possible ambiguity in the meaning of "from the recent losses of their husbands"? (¶ 6)

(11) To what does "the found loot" refer ¶ 6?

(12) How many potential victims are there in this incident according to ¶ 7? How many were there (for the same incident) according to ¶ 3?

(13) What is going to happen to the "found loot"?

(14) To what does "security" refer in ¶ 7?

(15) What bit of instructive writing is there in ¶ 9?

(16) Who winds up being suspected in ¶ 10?

Article #3

November 10

BAIL SLASHED TO $4 MILLION IN COMPUTER THEFT CASE

(1) A U.S. magistrate, speculating that computer expert Richard Stanley still may have control of more than $2 million in unrecovered funds from a $10.2 million bank swindle, Wednesday lowered his bail from $6 million to $4 million.

(2) "Two million dollars is still floating around somewhere," Magistrate Henry Crane said. "I'm not concerned whether it is in his possession. I'm concerned whether he has control over the money still adrift in the world."

(3) Stanley was arrested Monday in the computer theft of $10.2 million from Security National Bank October 25.

(4) When Stanley was arrested, police recovered thousands of polished diamonds with a wholesale value of $13 million, which Stanley allegedly bought from a Soviet diamond trading company in Switzerland with $8.145 million of the stolen funds.

(5) The judge said $2 million is still in European banks and had not been returned.

(6) The FBI Thursday said it located Stanley because he tried to recover a $6,000 advance he had paid to set up a diamond-selling business. When Stanley wanted the $6,000 returned, he gave a California post-office box number to a man in Rochester, N.Y.

(7) The Rochester man called the FBI after seeing Stanley's photograph on television.

(8) Meanwhile, a California newspaper reported at least two more people were involved in the scheme.

(9) The newspaper said Stanley was not the person who bought $8 million worth of diamonds from a Russian dealer in Geneva, Switzerland, with funds stolen from the Security National Bank.

(10) One of the Accomplices posed as a reputable Los Angeles gem dealer, the newspaper reported. The story said negotiations for the diamonds had begun more than two weeks before the money was illegally transferred out of a Los Angeles bank, allegedly by Stanley.

(11) Alexei Bonilav, director of the Russian jewel firm office for Western Europe, was quoted as insisting that neither of the two men he dealt with was Stanley.

Questions for Article #3

(1) What does the title promise the subject will be?

(2) What are the possible ambiguities in the title?

(3) Why did the U.S. magistrate lower Stanley's bail? (¶ 1)

(4) Is there any connection between the amount still missing and the amount the bail was lowered (¶ 1)?

(5) What is the significance of the magistrate's "concerns," and how does that logically affect his act of lowering the bail (¶ 2)?

(6) What is a "computer theft," according to the article? Were computers stolen?

(7) What do you suppose the Government will do with the $13 million worth of polished diamonds it has confiscated from

Stanley? Why has the author not included that in the article (¶ 4)?

(8) How are we to square the information in ¶ 5 with the statements in ¶ 2 concerning the whereabouts of the missing money?

(9) What, if anything, is confusing in ¶ 6?

(10) How does the information in ¶ 9 connect to the information in ¶ 4? Who "bought" the diamonds?

(11) What is the significance of the information in ¶ 10?

(12) What is the significance of the information in ¶ 11?

EXERCISE

Here is a fourth article, dealing with a problem of considerable proportions and of intense interest to the readers of that newspaper. The conference was widely publicized, and arguments continued long into the night on this and other equally controversial issues. Readers of this article, therefore, would have a keen interest in what happened, what was said, and what opinions carried the day.

Make a series of questions for this article similar to the questions for the previous three articles, and then answer them. Then, in a few sentences, paraphrase Dr. Shortup's view of the problem and his suggestions for its solution.

Article #4

PANEL AIRS TEACHER CONTRACTS

Discusses Issues of Negotiations

(1) Negotiations in public education in this state have gone full circle from a time when a negotiations act seemed imminent to a time when it seemed unlikely one would pass, the State Superintendent of Education said Saturday.

(2) Dr. Dalton Shortup keynoted the University's curcial "Issues in Education" conference. More than 200 educators, legislators, parent-teacher organization officials and board of education members attended.

(3) "State law extends to labor groups the right to bargain. Although not mentioned specifically, teachers and other

employee groups in the school districts in this state do bargain collectively. It is a fact of life. But to some it is still a distasteful and time-consuming practice that leads to dissension and conflict," Dr. Shortup noted.

No Identified Process

(4) He said part of the problem is that there is no identified process which may serve as a means to get employees and employers together, outlining the agenda resulting in settled agreements. Each district handles matters differently.

(5) People do agree that educators have the right to collectively bargain with employers for salaries and fringes, he emphasized. They also feel there should be a process for conducting the bargaining sessions and while mediation and fact-finding may need to be conducted by third parties, binding arbitration would be contrary to the best interests of local autonomy and sound education.

(6) What needs to occur, Dr. Shortup continued, is that a process for bargaining be developed in each district. "The more formal it can be, the more rigidly it can be followed and the more beneficial it would be in settling disagreements."

Notes Some Danger

(7) Citing the urgency of devising a workable bargaining process, the Superintendent noted that there is also some danger in concentrating too much on the process.

(8) "When it comes to satisfying all the actors on the scene of public education, one would have to conclude that the public has a substantial interest in what transpires. The bargaining process and the end result must consider the interests of the public because it is the public that pays the bill, the younger generation of the public which is directly acted upon by the system and society in general that is affected by what happens," he said.

(9) He noted the greatest concern of the public about collective bargaining in education is not simply whether employees are entitled to more salary and better working

conditions, but whether the process will improve or decrease the chances of developing an educational program adapted to the needs of the community.

Should Be State Function?

(10) Stressing the importance of local decision-making, Dr. Shortup noted that solutions to employer-employee relations and problems should be determined and implemented at the local level.

(11) Dr. Bill Bergen, executive secretary of the State Education Association, disagreed with Dr. Shortup in a panel discussion noting that because education is a statewide operation, it ought to be a state function.

EXERCISE

Find an article in your daily newspaper that suffers from the same kinds of problems as do the four articles considered in this chapter. Construct a series of questions to point out the weaknesses, answer them, and rewrite the article, assuming whatever knowledge necessary to fill in its gaps. Be sure that your article fulfills the promises that the original left unfulfilled.

Chapter VIII

INTRODUCTION TO CONSISTENCY

A. PERSUASION AND CONSISTENCY

Our legal system is based on the concept of precedent: Whatever the highest authority has previously judged to be a standard of fairness must hold in all cases that involve that standard. If every case was clear-cut, if all societal needs were constant and all circumstances unchanging, our courts would have little trouble in deciding how to handle any case that came before them. They would merely have to refer to precedent, where it existed, and decide the case before them so that it would remain consistent with past cases. Since, however, most cases are far from clear-cut, and since our societal needs and personal circumstances are always changing, courts must forever struggle to remain consistent with their previous decisions. Lawyers who find themselves faced with strong adverse precedents will try to persuade the court of one or more of the following:

(1) The present case can be distinguished from previous cases because of certain factors particular to it;

(2) Circumstances have so changed since the previous cases were decided that to apply the principles that produced justice in those cases would produce injustice in the present case;

(3) The precedents were decided on an erroneous principle, and the court should take this opportunity to overturn the existing principles of law in favor of ones more reasonable and just.

Lawyers can usually find some argument to make for a client because the circumstances of past cases rarely repeat themselves exactly and because new concepts of justice are constantly evolving, although always at the slowest of paces. In addition, if the matter is one that involves state law, one can usually find an example of some other state's having handled the matter differently. The advocate's job is to persuade the court to judge the situation from the vantage point of his or her client.

Chaim Perelman, one of today's leading theorists of law, defines formal or abstract justice as "a principle of action in accordance with which beings of one and the same essential category must be treated in the same way." [1] Our legal system aims at this ideal. If our legal standards are clearly articulated, consistently maintained, and adequately illustrated by the thousands of cases on record, then our citizens will know what they may or may not do in most situations. If our courts were to alter the law dependent on who was appearing before them or how they felt about a particular set of facts, then no one could rely on precedent and the legality of any action would depend entirely on the whims of whoever had the power to judge them.

The perfection of a system of precedents is, however, only an ideal. When societal attitudes change, our law must eventually alter to suit them. Moreover, most legal cases contain so many complexities, ambiguities, and questions, both of fact and law, that no one clear precedent can be found on which to base the entire decision. Cases that contradict each other abound, sometimes because individual courts differ in their views of what the law has been, and sometimes because other elements of the case persuaded the courts not to emphasize the one particular element that now appears in conflict.

It is not within the scope of this book to try to account for the conflicts and inconsistencies of our system of legal precedents. They are mentioned here only so that you will not be misled into believing that you can find a "right answer" for any of the problems and exercises that lie ahead. You should understand, as well, that legal education is concerned with training you how to think as clearly as possible and how to express yourself as cogently as possible, and these objectives are best accomplished by assuming the fiction of an ideal legal system, not by training you how to manipulate an imperfect one.

---

1. Chaim Perelman, *The Idea of Justice and the Problem of Argument,* (London: Routledge & Kegan Paul, 1963), p. 16.

In this chapter we shall concentrate on two problems of Persuasion: (1) how to recognize the difference between an argument and a conclusion; and (2) how to keep a series of related arguments consistent with one another. The second problem especially affects legal thinking and writing, for in a system of law based as ours is on precedent, a single decision can be seen as just only in relation to other decisions that deal with the same principles. You will be able to understand this more completely as we slowly trace the thought process of a series of decisions made by one student in response to the Exercise that follows. In order to benefit as fully as possible from the chapter, do the Exercise yourself before reading beyond it. Comparing your own responses with his will better enable you to analyze your own thought processes.

EXERCISE

The Law: "No left turn may be made onto Main Street from South Street. The Fine for an infraction shall not be less than $10 nor more than $100."

All of the following people broke the above law. As judge, how much would you fine each and why?

(1) A was speeding.

(2) B comes from a different state and has never seen that intersection before.

(3) C is a native of this city but has never driven through that intersection before.

(4) D did not know about the law and could not see the sign because the truck in front of him was blocking his vision.

(5) E had been drinking (alcohol) heavily.

(6) F made the turn at 4:00 A.M., when no one was in sight.

(7) G made the turn at 5:00 P.M. on a day when rush hour traffic was particularly heavy.

(8) H made the turn because the right hand turn was a road closed for repairs, and the street straight ahead was blocked by a truck which had broken down.

(9) J took the turn thirty minutes after H, just as tow trucks were starting to drive away with the disabled truck.

(10) K was transporting his pregnant wife, who was in labor, to the hospital on Main Street.

(11) L had been ticketed three times previously for the same offense.

(12) M made the turn at sunset, insisting later that the sun was in her eyes, preventing her from seeing the sign.

(13) N feared her transmission was about to fail and wanted to get to her mechanic's shop, located across the street from the hospital, as quickly as possible.

(14) P had the same problem and the same mechanic as N, but he had been warned for months that this danger was imminent. P is poor.

(15) Q has the same problem as P, except he is financially comfortable.

(16) R is in the same position as Q and is saving for a new boat.

(17) S is in the same position as Q, but she is saving for an expensive kidney operation for her ten-year-old son.

B. ARGUMENT V. CONCLUSION

The fines you levied on the seventeen drivers represent conclusions you came to concerning the relative seriousness of their infractions. Your responses to the question "Why?", however, should have been arguments, not conclusions. Were they? Can you distinguish between argument and conclusion while you are engaged in the writing process? Can you distinguish between them later on, when you reread what you have written? You cannot hope to be a completely competent lawyer without developing these abilities.

A conclusion is no more than a label. If a writer has constructed an argument carefully enough, it should lead the reader inevitably to one and only one logical answer or set of answers. Ideally, therefore, a writer should not ever have to articulate a conclusion, it should be such a natural and compulsory result of the argument. Good writers, however, will always spell out their conclusions, for purposes of emphasis, thoroughness, and a sense of closure. In other words, a conclusion, properly used, is no more than a rhetorical device to underscore for the reader the inexorable quality of the writer's logic and to inform the reader that the argument has come to an end.

Unfortunately, weaknesses like impatience, carelessness, over-confidence, or the lack of sufficient logic often tempt writers to forsake the process for the product, to jump to the conclusion without having articulated all the argumentative steps necessary to ensure its validity.

It is often no easy task to distinguish a conclusion from an argument, especially when the conclusion seems perfectly clear to you. You are so convinced by the evidence and logic you present that you confidently expect any intelligent reader to see the situation the way you do. You find yourself trapped in the position described at the beginning of Chapter II of this book (second paragraph), where the mere association of the words you have written with the thought you were trying to convey tricks you into believing that those words will adequately communicate with and convince your reader.

There are several tests that can help you discover how much a statement argues and how much it concludes, the best one being based on the theories behind the self-revision system explained in Chapter II. Look at the main verbs of the statement. Are they demonstrably weak? If so, the statement must tend towards the conclusive rather than towards the argumentative. (Remember, though, that no verb is weak or strong in and of itself, but only in its usage.) Weak verbs leave so much interpretive leeway to the reader that a writer who uses too many of them cannot hope to control the communication well enough to make a convincing argument. Instead of directing the reader's response, the prose will be merely asking the reader for acquiescence.

Example:

"Capital punishment should be abolished because it is morally reprehensible."

The main verbs are "should be" and "is"; since the sentence does not deal in establishing existences or suggesting equalities (the two strong uses of the verb "to be"), both verbs are weak. The statement does not argue why the death penalty should be considered morally reprehensible; it merely labels it as such.

Another example:

> "My client, Samuel Square, demands damages from the Paris Cinema because he feels disheartened by the lowering of public morality."

Once again the word "because" makes the mere conclusion that follows it sound like an argument. The verbs are "demands" and "feels." "Demands" does indeed capsulize the meaning of the first half of the statement and is therefore a strong verb. "Feels," however, by no means centers our attention on the importance of the thought of the second half (which, we must assume, should have something to do with "the lowering of public morality"). Does how Sam "feels" give him any right to collect damages? If he feels disheartened by his favorite baseball team losing a double-header, should he be allowed to demand damages from the ballclub? As in Chapter II, we see here how concentrating on the main verbs allows us to recognize quickly the strengths and weaknesses of a sentence. In the above example, a good thought may lurk beneath the surface, but it remains buried under elegant diction, facile rhythms, and a relatively sophisticated sentence structure.

Besides checking the main verbs, try these other methods of distinguishing argument from conclusion.

—Ask the question "Why?" of the statement. The more explaining that needs to be done to make sense of the statement, the more conclusory it was in the first place. Compare, for example, the following two statements:

(a) You should buy brand X cereal because Jocko Jones, the famous football player, recommends it.

(b) You should buy brand Y cereal because it contains 100% of the recommended daily allowance of fifteen essential vitamins and minerals.

Asking "Why?" of the first statement takes us further away from good reasons for buying cereal X. Should we buy X because Jones knows something about cereal? Does he recommend it because he eats it or because he is paid for it? Are his eating habits necessarily good ones for everybody? Asking "Why?" of statement (b), on the other hand, leads us directly into considerations of why one cereal might be better for us than another. How important are vitamins and minerals to us? What are the reasons for eating cereal in the first place?

—Juxtapose the statement with its negative. The more possible sense that can be made of the latter (the original's opposite), the more conclusory was the original. Examples:

> (a) (original): Capital punishment is morally reprehensible.
>
> (negative): Capital punishment is not morally reprehensible.

One can reasonably imagine either statement being made by a thoughtful person. Either statement could be argued with reason and force simply because neither makes an argument by itself. Both merely conclude or offer an opinion.

> (b) (original): You should buy brand Y cereal because it contains 100% of the recommended daily allowance of fifteen essential vitamins and minerals.
>
> (negative): You should not buy brand Y . . . .

The negative of the original would take a good deal of explaining to make it seem reasonable. Because it seems to defy logic, the original must have contained some persuasive logic, some explanation that made sense.

These tests are in some way all variations of each other, and none of them is foolproof. They can help you to discover how much thought has been expressed in the original statement, but not to prove or disprove it. Scrutinizing the main verbs for strength or weakness will help you uncover conclusions masquerading as arguments not only in someone else's prose, but also in your own. The process is a slow one, and it demands much patience from you. Impatience with your own writing of arguments will lead you to paste labels on crucial points instead of explaining their cogency.

Here now are responses made to the seventeen illegal left turn questions made by a student named Jeffrey who approached the assignment with earnestness and a sense of justice. See if you can detect when he is merely concluding instead of arguing the case for the fines he chose. We shall look at each of his responses in some detail.

Fines for Illegal Left Turns

1. Case: A was speeding.

   Response: I would fine A $100 because he was speeding. *$100.00*

2. Case: B comes from a different state and has never seen that intersection before.

   Response: Because B is from a different state, thus probably unsure of himself, I would give him the benefit of the doubt. *$10.00*

3. Case: C is a native of this city but has never driven through that intersection before.

   Response: Ignorance of such a law, beside the fact of the presence of a sign, provides no excuse. The law has been broken. *$35.00*

4. Case: D did not know about the law and could not see the sign because the truck in front of him was blocking his vision.

   Response: The situation sounds like the vehicle did not stop when reaching the intersection. *$50.00*

5. Case: E had been drinking (alcohol) heavily.

   Response: E's drinking of alcohol obviously requires the maximum fine, because of the possible consequences. *$100.00*

6. Case: F made the turn at 4:00 A.M., when no one was in sight.

   Response: The law has been broken. F knew what he was doing. *$50.00*

7. Case: G made the turn at 5:00 P.M. on a day when rush hour traffic was particularly heavy.

   Response: Making an illegal left turn during heavy rush hour traffic is a senseless, thoughtless act. It could have caused a terrific accident, or at least gummed up traffic for a while. *$75.00*

8. Case: H made the turn because the right hand turn was a road closed for repairs, and the street

straight ahead was blocked by a truck which had broken down.

Response: It appears from the facts that there was no other alternative. The fine should be minimal. *$10.00*

9. Case: J took the turn thirty minutes after H, just as tow trucks were starting to drive away with the disabled truck.

Response: The circumstances were in the process of being changed. J should have waited. *$40.00*

10. Case: K was transporting his pregnant wife, who was in labor, to the hospital on Main Street.

Response: K knew what he was doing. It was important to get her to the hospital the fastest way. *$10.00*

11. Case: L had been ticketed three times previously for the same offense.

Response: It appears that L does not take the law very seriously. This disregard for the law requires the maximum fine. *$100.00*

12. Case: M made the turn at sunset, insisting later that the sun was in her eyes, preventing her from seeing the sign.

Response: When a person is given a license to drive, she accepts the responsibility to be a responsible driver. What if it was not a sign she failed to see, but a person? *$60.00*

13. Case: N feared her transmission was about to fail and wanted to get to her mechanic's shop, located across the street from the hospital, as quickly as possible.

Response: N was forced to take the turn. She was in some danger already. *$20.00*

14. Case: P had the same problem and the same mechanic as N, but he had been warned for months that this danger was imminent. P is poor.

Response:	P should have taken care of the problem, but his poverty probably prevented him. Same as N. *$20.00*	
15. Case:	Q has the same problem as P, except he is financially comfortable.	
Response:	Q had no reason, like P did, not to take care of the car. Q was reckless. *$85.00*	
16. Case:	R is in the same position as Q and is saving for a new boat.	
Response:	The new boat is no excuse. *$85.00*	
17. Case:	S is in the same position as Q, but she is saving for an expensive kidney operation for her ten-year-old son.	
Response:	S has a better excuse than R, but not as good as P. *$45.00*	

C. RESPONSES TO THE LEFT TURN PROBLEM: PART I

The fines Jeffrey chose are all defendable, although he has not articulated those defenses for us most of the time. We can hear in his tone that he has given some thought to each and that he has tried hard to be neither extreme nor arbitrary. I asked him what standard he had used in assessing the fines. He told me that in all cases he had used one and only one principle: The more serious the violation, the higher the fine. I asked him how he defined "seriousness." He had no ready answer. When we examined closely each of his decisions, we found that within his vague principle of "seriousness" he had established many different standards, explaining little about any of them, and switching from one to another as the situation seemed to demand. Such procedures (or lack of procedures) lead inevitably to gross inconsistencies.

He felt at first that all seventeen were quite consistent. After all, each decision had come from his particular sense of justice, based on the same sensibilities, the same instincts. Even if consistency could be attained this way, however, a system of Law could not possibly hope to produce justice thereby. For a society to be able to rely on evenhandedness from its courts and legislatures, the interpretation of the laws must not be subject only to the whims of individual sensibilities. Reasons must be articulated, and arguments in one case must be applied with equal force to all other cases which raise the same kinds of questions. We found, however, that he had not been able to maintain consistency, even applying the same mind to only seventeen similar situations, and at one sitting.

We spent several hours going through the seventeen responses, trying to trace his arguments, to discover his standards, and to find some sense of consistency that would make sense of the relative harshnesses of the fines. In the following pages are summarized the main observations he and I made on the first twelve responses, dividing those observations into three categories:

(a) How much of each Response was argument and how much conclusion?

(b) What standards were used to come to each conclusion?

(c) In what ways is each consistent or inconsistent with the others?

Careful consideration of the large amount of detail offered here will help to clarify the problems involved and to suggest ways of avoiding these dangers in your arguments.

Case #1: A was speeding.
Response #1: *I would fine A $100 because he was speeding.*
          $100.00

(a) In this response Jeffrey makes no argument whatever, although the presence of the word "because" led him to think he had. He merely restates the facts he had been given and attaches a $100 price tag to them. No matter how much we might agree with him that speeders taking illegal turns deserve the highest of fines, we cannot pretend to know what his reasons are.

(b) He neither articulates not implies a standard behind his decision. A standard gives us a sliding scale to work with, something in the form of "The more _____, the higher the fine," so that we can judge each instance in comparison with other instances. Here we are given only a label: "speeding = $100." We can see the lack of standard (and lack of argument) more clearly, perhaps, if we exchange "speeding" for some non-pejorative term, for instance "British." The case then becomes, "A was British," and the response, "I would fine A $100 because A was British."

(c) At this point we have no other decisions to compare with and therefore no questions of consistency can be raised.

Case #2: B comes from a different state and has never seen that intersection before.

Response #2: *Because B is from a different state, thus probably unsure of himself, I would give him the benefit of the doubt. $10.00*   .

(a) Once again he repeats the facts given him: "B is from a different state." This time, however, he adds a label of his own, "unsure," presumably as an argument (notice again the presence of the word "because"), but actually as a conclusion. He gave driver B "the benefit of the doubt," but he did not explain for us what that "doubt" consists of or how we can use the concept in future cases. Perhaps the word "doubt" has something to do with the word "probably," but even so, he has still not done more than affix a label, then state a conclusion.

(b) Although he was not aware of it when writing this response, he offers us here a standard of judgment, one based on "sureness": "The more unsure a driver is about driving, the lower the fine." While agreeing that the standard was a logical extension of this decision-making process, Jeffrey recognized it was of questionable use in deciding many other cases.

We tried to uncover what he had meant by "unsure." It could hardly refer to the way in which the driver had operated the automobile, for that would lead to fining good drivers more harshly than incompetent ones, which makes no sense at all. He suggested that "unsure" had something to do with the driver's foreign status, with his ignorance of the intersection and the law which governed it. If so, however, that would produce another standard, based on awareness of the law: "the less aware of the law a driver is, the lower the fine." We agreed that no legal system would endorse this kind of thinking because it would put the knowledgeable citizen at a legal disadvantage and, at the same time, raise a great many problems of proof, since no one can know with confidence how "sure" someone else might have been at a given moment.

(c) Having been given no argument and no standard in Case #1, we could not check this case for consistency with the previous one. Neither of the standards implied gave any promise for consistent application in future cases.

Case #3: C is a native of this city but has never driven through that intersection before.

Response #3: *Ignorance of such a law, beside the fact of the presence of a sign, provides no excuse. The law has been broken. $35.00*

(a) First we applied the main verb test to each of the sentences. "Provides" turned out to be a weak verb, for Jeffrey thought the important material in the first sentence was "ignorance" and "excuse." "Provides" did no more than "is" would have done, merely equating "ignorance of the law" and "no excuse." The first sentence, then, states a conclusion but offers no argument to back it up.

The main verb of the second sentence, "has been," also turned out to be weak. (Remember that for these purposes the main verb in any passive construction is the verb "to be," the participle being considered only a verbal adjective.) He considered the concept of "breaking" the central interest here. Transforming the passive construction into an active form made the vacuity of the sentence more apparent: "C broke the law." This statement tells us nothing more than we already knew from the facts: The instructions for the Exercise informed us that "All the following broke the law." How then should the assertion that "The law has been broken" help us to understand his reasoning?

We also applied the negative restatement test to the first sentence, producing the following opposite statement: "Ignorance of such a law, beside the fact of the presence of a sign, provides an excuse." This made almost as much sense to us as the original had, suggesting that no argument had been articulated in the original.

(b) Jeffrey suggested that he had had another standard or sliding scale in mind when he qualified "ignorance of the law" with "beside the fact of the presence of a sign" (which he amended to "especially in light of the presence of a sign"): "The less reason a driver has to be ignorant of a law, the higher the fine." He refused to stand behind this as a workable standard on the basis that ignorance of the law should not excuse violations of the law, again because of the problems of proving just how ignorant the violator may have been at the time.

(c) We compared the result in #3 with that of #2 and discovered a glaring inconsistency. In #2 the driver had been fined the minimum, $10, because he had probably been ignorant of the law. In #3 the driver was fined three and a half times as much, and yet was presumably just as ignorant of the law. The presence of a sign is mentioned in #3, but that could hardly account for the difference in the fines, since the same sign would have existed for the driver in #2. Jeffrey seemed puzzled by his having differentiated between the two cases. He thought perhaps he had felt that an out-of-state driver would have had less opportunity to be familiar with the intersection, but that would lead us back again to standards of comparative ignorance, which we had agreed should have no force whatever. He then noticed that even if we accepted a standard of comparative ignorance, a good argument could be made for fining the driver C in #3 even less harshly than the driver B in #2, since we are told that C had never driven through the intersection before, but we have no such knowledge about B. He may have driven through there any number of times, despite his residency in some other state. The two fines started to appear arbitrary.

Case #4: D did not know about the law and could not see the sign because the truck in front of him was blocking his vision.

Response #4: *The situation sounds like the vehicle did not stop when reaching the intersection. $50.00*

(a) In place of an argument here we found an inference and an implication. The facts dealt with driver D's ability to see the sign, but Jeffrey's response dealt with whether or not the driver stopped at the intersection, something he must have inferred, since the facts do not mention it. Given this inference, he seems to have implied that D should be fined in the middle range because of what might have happened when he did not stop at the intersection. Jeffrey felt strongly that he had been getting at something important here, but he realized that he had not yet articulated what that was.

(b) In trying to articulate what his inference and implication had produced, he came up with the following standard: "The more dangerous the illegal turn, the higher the fine." This seemed to him a more reasonable standard, somewhat parallel in effect to his original, vague principle of seriousness of violation. He was tending towards defining "seriousness" as "potential for physical danger," a concept we could use on each of the cases before us.

(c) I asked Jeffrey why he had not referred to the "ignorance of the law" issue here as he had in the second and third cases, especially since the facts seemed to concentrate on it. At first he insisted that the danger issue had taken his attention away from it completely, but after a while he suggested that had he dealt with the ignorance issue, he would not have been able to justify the higher fine for D. Looking back, we saw that B, C, and D, all presumably equally ignorant of the law, were fined substantially differently ($10, $35, and $50).

If, on the other hand, we applied a "danger" standard and accepted the inference that driver D had not stopped at the intersection and further inferred that B and C had stopped, then we could justify giving D a higher fine than B's or C's; but note how far afield (in terms of inference and unstated arguments) we have to go to justify this. Jeffrey could hardly insist that all of this necessarily followed from the wording of his response.

Case #5: E had been drinking (alcohol) heavily.

Response #5: *E's drinking of alcohol obviously requires the maximum fine, because of the possible consequences. $100.00*

(a) We looked at the main verb, "requires," and found it weak, since Jeffrey identified "consequences" as the most important part of his sentence. He saw that by merely concluding that speeding deserves the maximum fine, he had made no reasoned argument, despite the extreme emphasis of "obviously" and "requires."

A word of warning: Never use the word "obvious" (or its cognates "surely," "of course," "certainly," etc.) without a personal qualification (e.g. "obvious to me"). There are only two possibilities: Either it was obvious to your reader, or it was not. If it was obvious, you have condescended to your reader by suggesting that you are embarrassed to have been forced to articulate such an apparent truth for the benefit of an unintelligent audience. If it was not obvious, your reader will concentrate on the question of obviousness instead of the substance of your comment. A hostile reader will stop to pick a fight on the issue of obviousness either out of sheer malevolence or in order to distract others from paying attention to what you really have to say. Writers often use these overly definite terms when they actually feel a good deal of uncertainty about their argument. An old adage instructs lawyers to use a threefold approach to legal argument: When the facts are not on your side, argue the law; when the law is not on your side, argue the facts; when the facts and the law are not on your side, bang on the table and yell like Hell. Both "obviously" and "requires" here sound like that banging and yelling. When you notice others using words like these, it will be worth your while to dwell on the statement long enough to discover what is missing from their argument. When you find yourself tempted to use words like these, stop and ask yourself what weakness in your argument is making you feel compelled to bang on the table at this point.

(b) Jeffrey suggested that the standard implied by "because of the possible consequences" resembled the "danger" standard of #4, perhaps widened a bit to include consequences other than physical danger: "The worse the possible consequences from the illegal turn, the higher the fine."

(c) If we compare #5 with #4 (two responses we have related to the same "danger" standard), we can find consistency only if the drinking driver has committed a misdemeanor twice as potentially dangerous ($100 instead of $50) as the driver who (it was inferred) did not stop before entering the intersection. Had he stated the standard explicitly, Jeffrey now felt, he would have been able to continue with reasons (arguments) why the driver in #5 presented twice as much potential danger as the driver in #4.

Case #6:   F made the turn at 4:00 A.M., when no one was in sight.

Response #6:   *The law was broken. F knew what he was doing. $50.00*

(a) The first sentence here echoes the last sentence in #3 and repeats its weaknesses. In the second sentence, the verb "knew" might seem to be strong, seeming again to refer to the question of ignorance of the law; but Jeffrey maintained he had been concerned not with the driver's ignorance, but with his intentions, in which case "knew" is a weak verb, and the sentence offers no argument.

(b) Jeffrey was suggesting a new standard here, one of "intent," but his mid-range fine, taken by itself, does not give clear enough indications of the standard's parameters. He had been trying to imply the following: "The more intentionally a driver breaks this law, the higher the fine."

(c) Inconsistency reigns in Case #6. Repeating the sentence he used in #3, he tells us again that "the law has been broken." It made no sense there, and it makes no sense here; but to increase the nonsense, in #3 it produced a $35 fine, while here it produces a $50 fine.

If "F knew what he was doing" implies a standard of "intent," then we have nothing in the previous five cases with which to compare for consistency. If, on the other hand, it were to further the "ignorance of the Law" standard, then #6 appears somewhat consistent. Driver B, the out-of-stater, was fined only $10 because he had little reason to know what he was doing. Driver F in the present case knew exactly that he was doing, and therefore a fine five times as large does not seem unreasonable or inconsistent.

Case #7:   G made the turn at 5:00 P.M., on a day when rush hour traffic was particularly heavy.

Response #7:   *Making an illegal left turn during heavy rush hour traffic is a senseless, thoughtless act. It could have caused a terrific accident, or at least gummed up traffic for a while. $75.00*

(a) The weak verb in the first sentence once again indicates a conclusion unsupported by argument. He has merely labeled the rush hour turn with the adjectives "thoughtless" and "senseless," expecting that we will agree. We could disagree if we wished to, however, arguing that especially at rush hour one would have to think about such a turn carefully and would take it only if it made some kind of sense to do so. As long as he does not use strong verbs to tell us how to interpret his labels, he runs the risk of having us interpret them differently from his intentions.

In the second sentence, however, he offers us the beginnings of solid arguments (despite his misuse of the impoverished word "terrific"). A look at his main verbs, "could have caused" and "(could have) gummed up," tells us at least something about his main concerns. We disapprove of illegal turns not because of what they are, but because of what they do: They cause accidents and gum up traffic.

(b) We can imply four separate standards in his response:

(1) The more senseless the illegal turn, the higher the fine.

(2) The more thoughtless the illegal turn, the higher the fine.

(3) The greater the probability that the turn will cause an accident, the higher the fine.

(4) The greater the probability that the turn will obstruct the flow of traffic, the higher the fine.

The first two, which stem from labels instead of from arguments remain undefined and therefore impractical to use. They both suggest that the driver's state of mind determine the extent of the fine, and yet a judge would have little way of proving or disproving a defendant's assertions of conscious intent. The second standard poses a problem in logic as well: Are we to understand that the more the driver thinks about the illegal turn, the less he will be fined?

The second two standards, however, offer some help. He needs still to develop them in more detail, but both of them help to define what he meant by his original statement: The more serious the violation, the higher the fine.

(c) The "senseless" and "thoughtless" standards, impractical as they are in themselves, also conflict with the standard suggested by Case #2: "The more unsure a driver is about driving, the lower the fine." The standards here suggest the opposite: The more sure, sensible, and well thought out the driver's actions were, the lower the fine will be. All three standards were produced from conclusive statements. We see here evidence of the kinds of problems produced by multiple conclusions in a total absence of argument.

The "accident probability" standard in #7, though, agrees well with the "danger" standard of #4 and the "possible consequences" standard of #5. All three produced medium to high fines, depending on the seriousness of what might have happened as a result of the illegal turn. Jeffrey had articulated none of this, but he was beginning to see that something had indeed remained consistent in his mind as he assigned the various fines. To develop a workable principle he would have to explain how these three related to each other and why the fines differed.

He had overlooked one issue pertinent to consistency altogether. Driver F (#6) made the turn when no one was around; driver G (#7) made the turn when traffic was at its worst. How do these conditions affect their fines if at all? In order to explore that issue, he would have to construct a new category of "driving conditions," which would then have to be taken into account in all future decisions. You cannot begin to talk about consistency in matters of pears and apples until you call them both fruit.

Case #8:   H made the turn because the right hand turn was a road closed for repairs, and the street ahead was blocked by a truck which had broken down.

Response #8:   *It appears from the facts that there was no other alternative. The fine should be minimal. $10.00*

(a) Once again his weak main verbs indicate he had stated only his conclusion, without giving us his argument. Applying the "Why?" test produced interesting results in this case. Why should the fine be minimal in cases where there are no alternatives to breaking the law? Jeffrey argued in response—(notice, he argued) —that when one, through no fault of his own, is put in a position where any action would be illegal, then the action which produces the fewest or least serious consequences should be allowed by the Law. When we followed this argument further, we found it parallel to the reasoning in back of the self-defense exception to the laws of murder. If someone is about to murder you, you may murder them if there is no alternative action that would preserve your life. The Law says that as long as a life must be lost due to foul play, you are not required to let it be your own. Applying this thinking to this case would result in no fine at all, a reasonable conclusion to a convincing argument.

(b) Jeffrey felt that no sliding scale or standard emerged from his response to this case. He had not intended to suggest by his minimal fine that the fewer the alternatives there were, the lower the fine should be. Instead he had wanted to single out the one extreme case in which there was no alternative whatever.

(c) If for some reason our argument for no fine whatever could not be used, how would the driver in this case fare under the standards implied by some of the earlier cases? How consistent would they be in producing answers for driver H?

Under the "danger" standard of #4, we could argue reasonably for many different levels of fine, depending on the conditions at the time and the manner in which H took the turn. If H turned left with great caution, keenly aware of the exceptional circumstances, we could make a strong case for a minimal fine, because H would have actively decreased the danger of the turn. The same kind of reasoning could be used for the "possible consequences" standard in #5 and the "accident" standard in #7.

Under the "traffic flow" standard of #7 we could make another strong argument, that by not moving at all (H's only alternative to taking the illegal turn) he would have obstructed traffic far more than he did by taking the turn. He thus obeys the spirit of the law by breaking the letter of the law.

Under the "intention" standard of #6, however, we would be forced to argue for the opposite result, a higher fine. Driver H broke the law with the fullest of intentions, and under this standard therefore deserves the maximum fine. When a standard is capable of producing a ridiculous result, we must discard it, lest it also lead to injustices in more subtle cases, where we might not notice the illogicality as easily.

Case #9: J took the turn thirty minutes after H, just as tow trucks were starting to drive away with the disabled truck.

Response #9: *The circumstances were in the process of being changed. J should have waited. $40.00*

(a) The verb "should have waited" seems forceful enough, but when we look at his answer to the question why J should have waited, we find only the verb "were" (in the first sentence of the response). Jeffrey was now able to build with some ease an argument that tied into the argument for #8: In just a few moments the tow trucks would have removed the truck and thereby the necessity for drivers to choose one or another of the illegal alternatives. Since #8 produced an extreme "no alternative" exception rather than a sliding scale standard, case #9 would have no relation to case #8 once the truck was removed. We should then judge driver J by the others of our standards that might apply.

(b) He had implied no standard in Response #9, but his second sentence suggests a need for one: In a situation like this, how long does a driver have to wait before it becomes "necessary" for him or her to take an illegal turn? As the quotation marks imply, such a standard would help force us to define "necessity." You can begin to see how following through on one argument will lead to the unearthing of other problems that require yet more arguments.

Case #10: K was transporting his pregnant wife, who was in labor, to the hospital on Main Street.

Response #10: *K knew what he was doing. It was important to get her to the hospital the fastest way. $10.00*

(a) We have seen these main verbs before; they tell us no more now than they did then.

Jeffrey now was able to point out by himself how many times he had pounded on the table instead of making an argument: "E's drinking of alcohol obviously requires the maximum fine"; "The fine should be minimal"; "J should have waited"; and now "It was important . . . ."

It is not hard to imagine what was intended by "It was important to get her to the hospital in the fastest way," because this particular context offers such a dramatic association for those words; but what happens when we distance them a bit? What did Jeffrey mean by "the fastest way"? What else could be meant by the same phrase? If Response #10 became law, would an expectant father be able to drive across a mall or on a sidewalk or down a one-way street in order to get to the hospital, as long as he could prove that had been "the fastest way"? Would this new law protect him from a suit for wrongful death were he to kill a pedestrian by driving on the sidewalk? or by taking an illegal left turn?

(b) Jeffrey had trouble clarifying what standard he had been using in this case. He felt it had something to do with the emergency quality of the situation, but that the standard "The greater the emergency, the lower the fine when you break the law" would lead to all sorts of problems. Who is to judge the difference between convenience, seeming emergency, grave emergency, and the like? The driver? The police? The judge? Even after much thought he was still unwilling to formulate a standard from this case.

(c) Response #10 presented us with the single most glaring inconsistency to this point. Driver K is to be fined the minimum because "He knew what he was doing," and yet driver F in Case #6 (the 4:00 A.M. situation) was to be fined five times as much because "He knew what he was doing." Communication breaks down completely with this kind of double-talk, words that mean what the writer wants them to mean at that instant only, soon to be used again with totally different results. We have encountered this rhetorical practice before (cf. Humpty Dumpty's pronouncements, Chapter III, p. 46 ff.).

Case #11: L had been ticketed three times previously for the same offense.

Response #11: *It appears that L does not take the law very seriously. This disregard for the law requires the maximum fine. $100.00*

(a) The lack of argument here parallels that in Response #5: "E's drinking of alcohol obviously requires the maximum fine," although in that case "possible consequences" were mentioned as the basis for conclusion instead of "disregard for the law." Any abstract noun could be used as the subject for the verb "requires," and they all would leave us with no more than an opinion.

(b) He found he had implied a new standard here, one of "a lack of high seriousness": "The less seriously the illegal driver regards the authority of the Law, the higher the fine."

(c) One interesting consistency surfaced: Whenever Jeffrey had used the verb "requires," he had assigned the maximum fine. If he could only discover the origin of the sense of compulsion that accompanied his invoking of the maximum fine (he included Case #1, where he might as well have used "requires"), then he would be able to define one end of the spectrum of left turn violations that was starting to emerge from all of this juxtaposing of individual cases.

How do you imagine others of the cases would be resolved under this new "disregarding of the law" standard? Would driver F of Case #6 (the 4:00 A.M. situation) still receive a $50 fine? Would K, the expectant father in Case #10, still receive a $10 fine? What of the drinker, or the speeder, or the stymied driver?

Case #12: M made the turn at sunset, insisting later that the sun was in her eyes, preventing her from seeing the sign.

Response #12: *When a person is given a license to drive, she accepts the responsibility to be a responsible driver. What if it was not a sign she failed to see, but a person? $60.00*

(a) This response comes closer than any of the previous ones to making an argument, as we might guess from the strength of two of the four verbs, "accepts" and "failed." Here Jeffrey had been weighing the acceptance of responsibility on the one hand against the failure to act responsibly on the other. Such comparisons can produce meaningful answers, or at least indicate promising avenues of discovery. Without being aware of it, he was using on himself a favorite technique of so many legal educators, the Socratic method. He took an established case (the sun preventing her from seeing the sign) and changed one fact (substituting a person for the sign) to see how well the theory in question would hold up. Law students are put through these paces over and over in the course of their education. Just as soon as a particular theory seems established, the professor changes the hypothetical facts, and the theory cracks and crumbles. If legal educators use this technique to enlighten their students, then the same method ought to prove useful for self-examination.

(b) He implies here yet another standard: "The less responsible a driver is of the safety of others when making illegal turns, the higher the fine."

(c) This new standard conflicts with the "ignorance of the law" standards, but by this time we had agreed that the latter was unacceptable, so the conflict proved meaningless.

The "responsibility" standard fit well with all the others, even making some sense out of the "senseless" and "thoughtless" standards that looked so weak in #7.

We now had more than enough material to try to unravel exactly what he had meant by the "seriousness of the violation" and how all of these seemingly disparate decisions fit together. We decided to co-ordinate our thoughts, after which we could return to Cases #13 through #17.

D. DISCOVERING PRINCIPLES

The student whose thoughts we have been reviewing had treated the Exercise with due seriousness and had given a substantial amount of time and thought to it. If his answers appear to us oversimplified, we must not attribute it to a lack of effort or to a lack of intelligence, but rather to his failure to understand his own thoughts well enough to articulate them clearly for us.

We pieced together a great deal of his unarticulated thought from patterns that appeared in his choice of fines, in his choice of words, and in the relationship between the two. They had already produced for us several standards of decision-making. Juxtaposing those standards made it more easy for us to perceive their interrelationships. (Numbers refer to the Cases from which they came.)

#2(a) The more unsure a driver is about driving, the lower the fine.

#2(b) The less aware of the law a driver is, the lower the fine.

#3   The less reason a driver has to be ignorant of a law, the higher the fine.

#4   The more dangerous the illegal turn, the higher the fine.

#5   The worse the possible consequences from the illegal turn, the higher the fine.

#6   The more intentionally a driver breaks this law, the higher the fine.

#7(a) The more senseless the illegal turn, the higher the fine.

#7(b) The more thoughtless the illegal turn, the higher the fine.

#7(c) The greater the possibility that the turn will cause an accident, the higher the fine.

#7(d) The greater the probability that the turn will obstruct the flow of traffic, the higher the fine.

#11   The less seriously the illegal driver regards the authority of the Law, the higher the fine.

#12   The less responsible a driver is of the safety of others while making illegal turns, the higher the fine.

Somewhere entangled within these standards lay a principle or a set of connecting principles that he had used to judge the comparative seriousness of the infractions.   On close inspection the standards seemed to fall under four rubrics:

(a) Standards relating to the possibilities of danger from taking illegal turns (##4, 5, 7c, 12);

(b) Standards relating to the disruption of traffic flow that could be caused by illegal turns (##5, 7d);

(c) Standards relating to the importance of obeying all laws (##7a, 7b, 11);

(d) Standards relating to the driver's knowledge of the law and the driver's intent while taking the illegal turn (##2a, 2b, 3, 6, 7a, 7b).

1.   TURNS WHICH INCREASE THE POSSIBILITY OF DANGER

We found that he had actually been quite consistent in his fines when he had been considering potential danger as the significant standard.   Drivers D and M, both of whom could not see the sign (one being blocked by a truck, the other by the rays of the setting sun), might easily have caused accidents, since they were not as visually aware as they ought to have been while operating an automobile.   To both of these he had assigned medium range fines ($50 and $60), perhaps suggesting that a substantial warning was necessary to awaken their vigilance in the future.

To driver E, the heavy drinker, he had assigned the maximum fine, $100.   What was the difference between this case and that of drivers D and M, above?   By drinking heavily and thus reducing his reflex abilities, E had substantially increased the possibilities for causing an accident.   A moderate driving problem in front of him might have turned into a major disaster because he would have needed so much extra time to respond to it. We found we could apply the same logic to A, the speeder, who also would have less time than is reasonable to respond to an emergency. Note that Jeffrey had given A the maximum fine, as well.

Now we were getting somewhere. We had the makings of a standard that could be applied in all cases and would produce solutions to many of the problems involved. Taking an illegal left turn at any time and in any situation would increase the possibility of an accident happening: Other motorists would not be expecting the driver to turn there; pedestrians accustomed to using that intersection might not be looking in that direction; and drivers in back of the turning vehicle might be confused and startled. Thus any driver taking an illegal left turn (with perhaps an exception made for cases of necessity) should have to pay some fine because his or her act threatens others' safety; but the more the driver's behavior increases the possibility of danger, the higher that fine should be.

When this standard is applied to the first twelve situations, some of the fines become clearer and more defendable. The maximum $100 was given to driver A (the speeder), driver E (the drinker), and driver L (the three-time loser). Speeding, drinking, and cavalier disregard of the law (which produces overconfidence in the driver and adds to the number of potentially dangerous incidents) all dramatically increase the odds that some mishap will occur. Since they produce in the extreme exactly those situations that the law was trying to prevent, the extreme of the penalties allowed by the law ought to be invoked.

Drivers B, C, D, and M, all of whom (for different reasons) professed not to know about the regulation, also created hazardous driving situations, but they had not done so in as reckless a manner as A, E, and L. Their not being aware of the intersection's traffic pattern might endanger others, but they would be better prepared than A, E, or L to cope with a dangerous situation, should one arise, because they would be more in control of themselves and their vehicles. He had fined this group as follows: B, $10; C, $35; D, $50; and M, $60. Why did he fine B so much less than the others? He suggested that he was trying to temper justice in this case with courtesy, holding a guest from another state to a less strict standard than the local residents. Our new-found principle, this demonstrates, will not produce pat answers, but at least we will understand better the grounds on which we are arguing.

Drivers F and G (4:00 A.M. and 5:00 P.M.) posed some difficulty for him. If danger were the only standard, then he could argue for a lower fine for F, since no one was around to be endangered, and also for the ultimate fine for G, since rush hour is the most crowded and therefore potentially the most accident producing time of the day. Taking a different approach, he could also argue the opposite, that F should be fined even higher than G. F, expecting that no one would be on the street at 4:00 A.M., might not notice a darkly clothed pedestrian who, in turn, might be confident that F would not make a left turn; G, on the other hand, might redouble his vigilance as he took the turn because rush hour presents so many dangers all by itself. No matter what kind of answers might result from this type of inquiry, at least Jeffrey had begun to argue from the facts and to base his points on explicit theories, instead of merely stating conclusions based only on his instincts.

He had given H, the stymied driver a $10 fine. He could now argue that the illegal left turn presented only a minimal danger, since traffic was already aware that things were not in their usual state. Everyone would have been slowed down because of the jam, and anyone who could see what was happening would recognize that a left turn or a U-turn was a reasonable, although technically illegal, response. Driver J, who happened by while the tow trucks were starting to move, might deserve his higher fine ($40) because the ensuing commotion would cause uncertainty enough without drivers' taking illegal left turns at the same time, causing yet more opportunity for accidents.

This left only K, the expectant father. Applying the danger standard, Jeffrey could now argue convincingly for a minimal fine. The law is concerned with saving lives and preventing mishaps. Driver M took the illegal turn for that same purpose, in this case to protect the welfare of his wife and new child. He had balanced the possibility of harm from taking the turn against the possibility of harm from driving around the block, and he had opted for the former. He had obeyed the spirit of the law even as he broke the law. He could also argue for a much stiffer fine (although he preferred the lower one): K's wife and child were already in some danger, and to put them in yet greater danger by taking an illegal turn, especially in his highly anxious state, was to act rather recklessly. Again neither answer incontrovertibly solves the problem, but both represent reasonable thinking, arguments which can be tested and weighed against each other and against other decisions concerning illegal turns, producing dialogue from which reasonable decisions can be made.

Danger, then, seemed to us a workable standard for this problem. The regulation was intended (at least in part) to ensure greater safety at the intersection, and any behavior which exacerbates the possibility of danger should be dealt with according to its probability of producing dangerous consequences.

2. TURNS WHICH IMPEDE THE FLOW OF TRAFFIC

His second rubric, the disruption of traffic flow, seemed equally reasonable, but not quite as weighty. We mind traffic becoming snarled, but not as much as we mind lives being endangered. Since traffic control is another major reason for prohibiting left turns, we cannot ignore it as a factor in deciding upon fines for drivers who make illegal left turns. In some cases it could alter a decision we might have made using danger as the only variable.

It could, for example, cost driver B more than $10 if the argument was made that out-of-staters, unfamiliar with local traffic regulations, should practice even more diligence in reading traffic signs than the people who live in the area. For another example, G, the rush hour driver who might argue how his enhanced vigilance would reduce the chances of having an accident, could find his argument beaten down and his fine jacked up by the argument that his illegal turn exacerbated an already difficult traffic situation.

In dealing with both the danger standard and the traffic standard, we have found ourselves asking a pertinent question: For what purposes was the left turn law passed in the first place? If we know the principles behind the law, we can determine fines by asking how severely a particular infraction threatened precisely those things (safety, smooth traffic flow) the law had set out to protect. Jeffrey had been trying to use this kind of measuring device in his considering how "serious" each violation was; but since he had not been able to define what he meant by "serious," he never discovered a workable principle.

3. OBEYING THE LAW BECAUSE IT IS THE LAW

The third rubric concerns laws in general, not merely this particular one: Laws should be obeyed just because they are laws, no matter how a given situation might appear to the individual at the time of the violation. While it is true that everyone in these examples broke the law to some extent, some showed less regard for Law than others. For the cases in which this disregard was demonstrated in the extreme, a principle concerning willful disobedience might have been enough to raise the level of the fine, no matter how smoothly the traffic kept on flowing.

This principle might well affect the fines given to drivers F, H, and L. Drivers like F, who take illegal turns at 4:00 A.M., might not be endangering anyone or disrupting traffic, but they are displaying a conscious disregard for the law in assuming that their judgment is more to be trusted than the law is to be obeyed. If a judge sensed that F needed reproving on this issue, then he or she would be justified in raising the fine on that basis alone.

H, the stymied driver, on the other hand, showed little disrespect for the law by making the illegal turn, since nothing but illegal options were available. H could argue that he was trying to obey the laws but was unable to do so because of circumstances, an argument that might prevail with the officer on the street as well as the judge in a court.

L, the three-time offender, represents the other extreme. All citizens are presumed to be aware of posted signs; but one who has been ticketed for a specific offense three times previously has been proved to be most painfully aware of such a sign. Giving L the maximum fine, especially if the possibilities of danger or disrupting the traffic flow were not serious, would make a symbolic statement, reaffirming the Rule of Law. (It matters not for our purposes whether L is a person likely to understand that statement or learn from it. We are concerned only with the appropriateness of the size of the fine.)

4. KNOWLEDGE AND INTENT

The first three rubrics, then (danger, traffic, obedience), all seem reasonable and useful for forming arguments about the size of fines for violations. The fourth, concerning the driver's knowledge and intent, works far less well. A court can never be certain, or even convinced 2beyond a reasonable doubt, of what was in the mind of a defendant at the time of an illegal act. The defendants themselves may not understand or remember what their knowledge or frame of mind was at the time of the incident. How can we know whether the expectant father actually did weigh the danger of taking the turn against the danger of not taking it?

Other problems of proof confuse the matter even further. How can we know that a certain out-of-state driver has never been at that particular intersection before? or that the sun was actually in M's eyes? or that a truck was actually blocking D's view of the sign? When a court feels it cannot get close enough to the truth no matter what resources it uses, it usually avoids that kind of questioning altogether, if it possibly can. We can discard the fourth rubric, then, as being too difficult to apply in any given situation.

5. THE FINAL PRINCIPLES

We are left, then, with three principles, all of which must be considered in any illegal left turn case:

(1) The more the driver's actions endanger others and create possibilities for accidents, the higher the fine.

(2) The more the driver's actions threaten to interrupt the smooth flow of traffic, the higher the fine.

(3) The more the driver's actions indicate a gross disregard of the Rule of Law, the higher the fine.

The first two are based on the presumed purposes for the existence of the law; the third concerns the efficacy of all laws.

The process of assigning fines in this situation, then, becomes a process of weighing and balancing. How much weight do we want to give each of the three principles in general? In what kinds of situations should we shift that balance? How does one situation compare to another that has already been decided? How will a situation in the future be affected by the decision we are making at the moment? All of these considerations require forceful and coherent arguments from the lawyers involved. Pounding on the table and yelling "I win" will not help to clarify the situation.

E. RESPONSES TO THE LEFT TURN PROBLEM: PART II

Let us return now to Cases #13 through #17 to see of what help the three principles can be.

Case #13: N feared her transmission was about to fail and wanted to get to her mechanic's shop, located across the street from the hospital, as quickly as possible.

Response #13: *N was forced to take the turn. She was in danger already. $20.00*

Jeffrey's original response conflicted with his response to #8, where H, the stymied driver, was forced to take the turn and was fined only $10. What can we argue now?

In terms of danger, we might make the same argument as we made for the expectant father, that N was weighing one kind of danger against another and should be fined the minimum as a result. We might argue on the opposite side that people with failing transmissions should be even more careful not to make illegal turns, since their cars are more likely to break down and create even more opportunities for accidents. Although this latter argument does not seem completely convincing on the subject of danger, it improves in strength when the question of traffic flow is considered.

Considering the Rule of Law principle, we could argue that emergency situations often reduce the moral culpability of someone breaking a law. On the other hand we could argue that in situations where machinery threatens to malfunction, users of the machinery should redouble their efforts to follow all regulations, lest the difficulties of the situation become magnified.

Confusing? It should be, for this case is full of ambiguities. Many fines, based on many different reasons, could be considered reasonable and fair.

Case #14: P had the same problem and the same mechanic as N, but he had been warned for months that this danger was imminent. P is poor.

Response #14: *P should have taken care of the problem, but his poverty probably prevented him. Same as N. $20.00*

Once again Jeffrey had based his decision on a standard of necessity, raising the same problems and inconsistencies as in the situation with N, above.

How does P compare to N? On the danger standard he fares much worse. N had been dealing with an unforeseen danger; P knew all along that something like this was bound to happen. P was endangering lives merely by driving his car, and taking an illegal left turn might well have made things worse. If P is too poor to fix his car, then, we could argue, he is too poor to use his car. (To convince yourself of this, substitute a state government for P and a nuclear reactor for the car.) P knows, moreover, that he will cause a traffic hazard eventually unless he fixes the car, and he must be especially wary of that possibility as he drives the last few miles to his mechanic's.

P also seems more culpable than N in his lack of regard for the law. The only law she risked disobeying was the one left turn she took. He risked the necessity of breaking a law every time he drove his car during the several months he was aware of transmission problems. She was presented with an immediate problem and had to make a quick decision. His putting off the repairs makes his illegal left turn look almost premeditated. Whatever fine we decide upon for P, it seems it should be greater than the one we choose for N, because P fares worse under all three principles.

Case #15: Q has the same problem as P, except he is financially comfortable.

Response #15: *Q had no reason, like P did, not to take care of the car. Q was reckless. $85.00*

Under the danger and traffic principles, we cannot differentiate between P and Q. They drove equally faulty cars, and they were equally aware of the potential for a breakdown in the near future. They also demonstrated an equal lack of regard for the left turn law's importance, for they both chose to take a shortcut to their mechanic's despite the traffic regulation. Neither of them should have risked the turn, knowing that they could lose control of the car at any moment. On what, then, could the great difference in fines ($20 for P, $85 for Q) be based?

Nothing in the three principles seems to justify this kind of variance. Do we need a fourth principle? or is there something wrong with the financial distinction he has drawn?

Under our Anglo-American judicial tradition, we attend foremost to the deed done and not to the person who did it. At first glance this would seem to be the ideal system. We disregard all personalizing elements (race, creed, background, financial status, sex, age, etc.) and concentrate on whether the act was legal or not. After ascertaining guilt or liability, we then give the judge some leeway by allowing for a spectrum of penalties. In practice, however, the system has often been found lacking, and we have compromised by the identity of the defendant first and his or her act afterwards.

The Soviet Union uses exactly the opposite system, judging each act in the context of who did it. They too have found it necessary to compromise, and, like us, now have a system that combines the two, however precariously.

On the one hand we must recognize that the level of fine chosen is a symbolic statement by the judge (cf. the case of driver L, p. 42 above). On the other hand we must be wary of the rampant subjectivity that threatens to take over when we abandon well-argued principles for the sake of individualized symbolic utterances.

Jeffrey had allowed the differential in financial status between P and Q to cloud the issue. Should P be allowed to cause more driving hazards than Q just because P is poor? On which should we be concentrating: Why they took the turns, or why they neglected to fix their automobiles? Does labeling Q "reckless" help argue this point?

Case #16:   R is in the same position as Q and is saving for a new boat.

Case #17:   S is in the same position as Q, but she is saving for an expensive kidney operation for her ten-year-old son.

Response #16: *The new boat is no excuse.* *$85.00*

Response #17: *S has a better excuse than R, but not as good as P. $45.00*

You can now see the weaknesses in his non-argumentative state-ment at first glance: the weak verbs, the labeling, the conclusory language and thought, the lack of reasoning. The issues here resemble those discussed above for cases ##13, 14, and 15. Under our three principles, there seems to be no difference in the situ-ations of P, Q, R, and S, unless we can add together an ability to fix an ailing car with a failure to do so and come up with a gross disregard of the law. Should a judge spend time and effort evaluating the uses to which defendants put their salary checks? If we encourage our judges to be swayed by issues like R's new boat versus S's son's kidney operation, how can we then tell them not to consider other personal characteristics such as charisma, sex appeal, or community status? (Once again we find the Socratic method, the "What if . . . ?" method, taking over.)

Jeffrey's seventeen responses failed to communicate to us the bases for his decision-making process because he had not yet figured it out for himself. Yet on close inspection most of his fines turned out to be reasonable and more or less consistent with each other, suggesting that he was using some kind of system, no matter how unconsciously. Criticizing the weaknesses in his writ-ing led us to discover the principles that had remained hidden to him.

The more we get away from writing facile conclusions, the more we can base our arguments on consistent theories, and the more interesting related issues seem to present themselves. We see again the impossibility of separating thought from expression of thought. Improving one will necessarily lead to improving the other.

Now you should be ready to tackle one of these large problems on your own. There are many ways of proceeding that eventually lead to good results. Here is one:

Step 1: Resolve each individual situation without too much reference to others.

Step 2: Compare your results, and look for inconsistencies.

Step 3: Group together all situations which seem to affect each other. (Note: One situation may reasonably belong in more than one group. Use each as often as necessary.)

Step 4: From these groups try to ascertain what general principles have been underlying your thought to this point. To get at this material, probe all weak verbs and attempt to explain fully all conclusions. Generate as many principles as the situation seems to require. You will be searching for answers to the question, "Why was this law made in the first place?".

Step 5: Revise all answers, articulating your reasoning process throughout and making consistency your main concern.

EXERCISE

Trespass

Preliminary definition: To be on the property of another without permission.

Task #1

All of the property owners in the examples that follow sue for trespass. The damages that a court may award can vary from $1.00 to $1,000. Which owners recover? Why? How much? Be sure that your answers are both reasonable and consistent.

(1) A stepped on B's front lawn inadvertently while taking a stroll.

(2) C walked across D's front lawn as a shortcut in her walk to work.

(3) E walked on a cement pathway across F's front lawn. The pathway connected Elm Street with Maple Street.

(4) G, a mailman, walked on a cement pathway to H's front door for the purpose of delivering the mail.

(5) J, a brush salesman, walked on a cement pathway across K's front lawn for the purpose of soliciting K's business.

(6) L, a religious missionary, walked on a cement pathway across M's front lawn for the purpose of trying to convert M. M had not invited L.

(7) N walked across P's corner gas station.

(8) Q drove across R's corner gas station.

(9) S walked across T's vegetable garden. T is rich.

(10) V walked across W's vegetable garden. W is poor and survives in part on the vegetables grown in the garden.

(11) X walked on Y's property without knowing it, thinking it was public property.

(12) Z hit a baseball from her own property across AA's lawn. The baseball landed on a vacant lot.

(13) BB swung on a rope attached to one of her trees, her path describing a circle, half of which was over CC's land. BB started from and ended on her own property.

(14) DD flew over EE's property on a hang glider at a height of 40 feet.

(15) FF flew over GG's property in a DC 10 at a height of 39,000 feet.

(16) HH built a fifth floor walkway from one of her buildings to another of her buildings across JJ's highway.

Task #2

Compose your own definition for Trespass, based on the knowledge you have gained from doing Task #1.

———◆———

At this point you may be starting to understand how all of the earlier discussion in this book of sentence structure, weak verbs, changing meanings for words, and the nature of the definition process fit into the argumentation process. The next exercise should give you a taste of how problems of definition and argumentation every bit as extreme and unrealistic as some of the ficticious exercises in this book await you in your future professional life.

EXERCISE

Using the decision below in Cumbo v. Cumbo as a starting point, generate ten other situations in which the term "family" could be at issue, and then carefully and thoroughly define "family," making sure that all ten of your cases are treated consistently and fairly when your definition is applied to them.

CUMBO v. CUMBO

Appellate Court of Illinois, First District, 1973.
9 Ill.App.3d 1056–1058, 293 N.E.2d 694–696.

PER CURIAM.

Susan Cumbo filed a complaint for divorce against Earle Cumbo and substituted service was had by service on Earle's 13-year-old brother, Gregory, who was at Earle Cumbo's residence on a two-year visit from Jacksonville, Florida, where he resided with his parents. After a default judgment had been entered against him, defendant appeared specially to quash service of summons on the ground that Gregory was not a "person of the family" of Earle Cumbo within the meaning of Chapter 110, sec. 13.2 of the Illinois Revised Statutes. The trial court denied defendant's motion and he brought this appeal.

The question involved in this appeal is whether the "member of the family" relationship contemplated by the statute necessarily involves some notion of permanence as to the residence at the defendant's usual place of abode by the said "member of the family."

Section 13.2 of the Civil Practice Act provides for substituted service as follows:

Sec. 13.2

Except as otherwise expressly provided, service of summons upon an individual defendant shall be made . . . (2) by leaving a copy at his usual place of abode, with some person of the family, of the age of 10 years or upwards, and informing that person of the contents thereof, provided the officer or other person making service shall also send a copy of the summons in a sealed envelope with postage fully prepaid, addressed to the defendant at his usual place of abode.

Plaintiff relies principally on Anchor Finance Corp. v. Miller (1956) 8 Ill.App.2d 326, 132 N.E.2d 81, when substituted service on defendant's sister in defendant's apartment was held valid. There, the sister and the defendant were held to be members of one family. The court found the following "admitted facts": that "the family lived in adjoining apartments in the same building" and the sister "spent considerable time" in the defendant's apartment where summons was served; and quoted from 72 C.J.S. Process § 48, p. 1060 that "such statutes presuppose that such a relation of confidence exists between the person with whom the copy is left and defendant that notice will reach defendant."

In Edward Hines Lumber Co. v. Smith (1961) 29 Ill.App.2d 35, 172 N.E.2d 429, the Second Dist. Appellate Court held that where the defendant resided in a rented room in a private residence, he was a member of the family of his landlord and service of the summons on Mrs. Keough, the landlord's wife was service on a "person of the family," defining "family" as: "A collective body of persons who live in one house, and under one head or manager; a household including parents, children and servants, and, as the case may be, lodgers or boarders." 29 Ill.App.2d 35 at 41, 172 N.E.2d 429 at 432. The court added (page 43, 172 N.E.2d page 432):

> "The defendant was not a mere temporary guest in the Keough home, but on the contrary, the evidence shows conclusively that he was a permanent resident in the Keough home and had been for some four or five years, and we believe that for the purpose of substituted service of summons the defendant was a member of the Keough family as contemplated by Section 13.2 of the Civil Practice Act."

In Sanchez v. Randall (1961) 31 Ill.App.2d 41, 175 N.E.2d 645, service upon a person, Mrs. Kellogg, who rented a bedroom in defendant's apartment, was held valid, the court stating, inter alia (at p. 49, 175 N.E.2d at p. 649): "She was not a temporary guest for she for all intents and purposes permanently resided in the home of the defendant," and held (page 50, 175 N.E.2d page 649) that "Mrs. Kellogg could properly be considered as a member of the family of the defendant."

Both in *Hines Lumber Co.* and in *Sanchez,* the negative inference is clear that a temporary guest in the defendant's usual place of abode is not a member of the family within the meaning of the statute. We do not think that, under the circumstances of this case, the fact that this temporary guest was related by blood to the defendant is enough to make him a member of the family for the purposes of the statute.

From these cases, then it is apparent that the notion of a permanent relationship is essential to the idea of a "family" within the meaning of Section 13.2 of the Civil Practice Act. Permanent residence in the home of the person sought to be served—or some rough equivalent as was present in Anchor Finance Corp. v. Miller, supra—is a requirement. Although Gregory Cumbo is related by blood to the defendant here, for the purpose of substituted service he was not a member of defendant's family at the time summons was served upon him.

The judgment of the Circuit Court of Cook County is reversed and the cause is remanded with directions to quash the service of summons and the default judgment be vacated and set aside.

Reversed and remanded with directions.

F.   INTRODUCTION TO COMPLEXITY

Cumbo v. Cumbo differs from the trespass and left turn cases in that the latter two concern issues that most of us can agree upon. To one extent or another we are generally in favor of private use of private land, of maintaining public safety, and of the orderly flow of vehicular traffic. Cumbo v. Cumbo, on the other hand, presents an issue for which we could find good arguments on either side. While the case is interesting, and dealing with it presents a significant challenge, few people will find themselves intellectually and emotionally gripped by its central issue. Most of us will find our own lives unaffected by it.

More complex difficulties arise, on the other hand, when we come upon a situation which does affect our lives and for which there are at least two strong and mutually exclusive arguments. Take for example the head-to-head conflict that has been raging for years between the environmentalists and the energy lobbies. All Americans would prefer cleaner air, safer natural habitats, more drinkable water, and all the other advantages of a healthy environment. At the same time all Americans would profit from a stronger energy program that would allow us to continue unlimited use of the automobiles, electric appliances, and petroleum products to which we have become so accustomed. If we cannot have both, but we still need and want both, how can anyone write a completely convincing argument in favor of one side at the expense of the other?

Several factors make writing about such issues extraordinarily difficult (as if writing were not difficult enough as is), but these two are among the most frustrating:

> (1) You can make a convincing argument, beautifully reasoned, based on well martialled, impeccably used facts, avoiding any trace of inference, and yet it still may not succeed in persuading anyone because the same kind of argument can be made for the other side; but

> (2) When you try to take into account the other side's argument, you encounter such severe organization problems and the crosscurrents of thought become so muddied that your previously streamlined argument can collapse under its own weight.

You will approach these writing tasks differently depending on what role you assume as writer. If you are counsel in a court case you will want to make the best argument for your side, showing the issues to be as one-sided as possible. If, however, you are writing a memo for your firm, you will want to explore both sides and perhaps suggest possible conclusions at the end. If instead you are writing to a client, you will probably want to focus on the conclusions, suggesting only the highlights of the reasoning that led you to them. Each task has its own difficulties and its own techniques for solving them.

Complex issues (those in which excellent arguments can be made for each of the conflicting issues involved) usually seem unresolvable. No one side can win conclusively because the opposite arguments refuse to fade away. It requires great energy, both emotional and intellectual, to perfect an argument for one side of such an issue, and that great involvement can mislead you into thinking that you are "right," that all intelligent people must agree with you once they understand the situation completely.

Whenever you feel this kind of overconfidence seeping into your veins, check yourself. Sit down calmly, and in a determined manner try to construct the best argument for the other side of the issue. It is a sobering experiment, but one that can keep you free from a kind of egoism that can destroy a lawyer's effectiveness. Work through the following hypothetical situation for practice.

A company has had a particularly good year and finds it has a surplus of $100,000. The Board of Directors decides that the money should be distributed to the workers of the company "in a just manner." Five plans are suggested:

(1) Give equal shares to all workers;

(2) Give larger shares to those who have been with the company longer;

(3) Give larger shares to those who have done better work;

(4) Give larger shares to those who show greater promise of future productivity;

(5) Give larger shares to those who have the greater needs for more money.

Each of these plans can be defended admirably, for each can be shown to produce some form of just recognition for the recipients; but, paradoxically, therein lies the injustice of choosing any one of them, for deciding on one will necessarily negate many of the good points of the others. If we can argue convincingly for rewarding many years of service to the company, and at the same time argue just as convincingly that those who have more need should receive more money, we will appear to be perpetrating injustice no matter what plan we choose, assuming that some of the neediest workers are also some of those who have not been with the company for long.

Weighing and balancing all five plans against each other can become hopelessly complex. On the other hand, arguing for one plan without comparing it to the other four would probably turn out to be logically inadequate. It is even possible that for most cases no one solution would work better than the other four. The rhetorical decision of how to form an argument may well depend on the practical considerations of what the Company hopes to accomplish by giving the bonuses.

If, for instance, the Company has been trying to foster a "one big happy family" image, then strong arguments can be made for the equal shares solution, and strong objections can be raised to each of the other four. In situations like these it is especially important to be aware of the distinction between Argumentation and Persuasion and to concentrate on the latter. Argumentation assumes that a right answer exists and attempts to reach it, in the name of truth. Persuasion ignores truth and cares only about getting the audience to agree. No one answer can be the right one in a situation like the one before us, although one answer may be the best one; in such cases, Persuasion, not Argumentation, is the proper rhetorical mode to use.

EXERCISE

For each of the following situations, decide which of the five bonus plans (on p. 220 above) would be the most appropriate and list the strongest arguments in favor of it. Then list the negative effects of not having chosen each of the other four plans.

(a) A manufacturer of widgets employs 500 people as manual workers, most of whom live in the small town in which the factory is located. Traditionally a percentage of the town's high school graduates take work in the factory and stay there for life. Labor conditions have never been much of an issue in the past, but more and more young workers have been talking about strikes for higher pay, and a few have been leaving the factory and taking the chance on finding work in the large industrial city 150 miles south. Management has $100,000 in bonus money to distribute.

(b) White Collar Corp. employs 5,000 people, almost all of them at desk jobs processing information. Much emphasis has always been placed on manifestations of status within the company (titles, location of desks, keys to executive washrooms, etc.), and a special task force has been created just to work on creating different schemes for work incentives (prizes for increases in work productivity, publicity for lack of lateness and absence from work, etc.). Substantial raises in salary usually are achieved only through promotion, and the company comprises so many different positions and ranks that promotion is a constant possibility. The Board of Directors has a $1,000,000 surplus to distribute as bonus money.

———◆———

Head to head combat between ideals generates perhaps the trickiest of writing problems, especially if you have to come to a resolution of the issues that seems fair to both sides. The following long Exercise is arranged for use in a classroom situation (over a period of several classes) but can be easily adapted for individual use.

EXERCISE

Part 1

Smedley is running for Congress against the incumbent, Horkenheimer. Smedley wants to attach a public address system to the top of his van and ride up and down the steets of the district telling people why they should vote for him instead of his opponent. Make an argument either for or against Smedley's being allowed to use a public address system in this way.

Here we have a head-to-head conflict between two important rights, free speech and privacy. On the one hand, Smedley should be allowed to say whatever he wants in the most effective way possible. On the other hand, other people have the right not to be bothered with loud, intrusive, and persistent noises promoting the interests of one individual. The problem in Part 1 is not how to resolve the question, but how to make the best argument for one side or the other. The rest of the Exercise demonstrates one possible process for resolving the issue.

Part 2

Make up a list of fifteen situations in which a sound amplification system might be used in a place frequented by the public.

Part 3

If you are in a classroom situation, form groups of three or four people, combine your lists of fifteen situations, and, as a committee, draft a regulation for the control of the use of sound amplification systems. Try to ensure that your regulation will function reasonably and justly for all the situations on your combined list. This may take several days' work.

Part 4

In class, exchange the regulation drafts between groups and share criticisms.

Part 5

In another class session, attempt to get unanimous approval on a final formulation of the regulation.

———◆———

You should discover through this process not only how hard it is to express yourself on a technical and complicated issue so that others understand what you intend to say, but also how completely right you can feel about a topic and yet still be far from agreeing with others who have given the same careful and thorough thought to the subject.

All this has been but a beginning. Significantly, the title of the final section of this book includes the word "Introduction," as does the title of the final chapter. Writing is a skill that continues to develop for as long as it is used. For most of us, writing never gets easier; we just get better at it. What is more, there seem to be no clear evaluation methods that will help us judge when "better" has become "good." If you wish to see whether you have become better at writing since the beginning of this book, do this final Exercise and compare your product to the one you produced for the first Exercise in the book (Sam Square v. the Paris Cinema), which dealt with the same general topic. The difference between the quality of the two essays represents how much "better" you have become.

EXERCISE

The Case of the Smouldering Smut Smiters

Herman Smutte started selling illegal drugs on street corners shortly before he was thrown out of Fair City High School for the last time. He subsequently spent three terms in reform school. He then changed professions and became a procurer. He abandoned that business when one of his employees was found murdered, and the police began pressuring him.

Smutte, 30 years old at the time, had amassed a good deal of capital through the years. He invested all of it in his next enterprise, Smutte Books, Inc. He chose a location on the street that separated the "porno area" of the city from the fashionable downtown shops. He kept his windows completely curtained and posted signs on the door and in the windows which read:

Smutte Books, Inc.

Pleasurable Reading for the Truly

Mature Adult

Browsers Welcome

but

Please do not enter if sexually frank

material is offensive to you!

He divided the shop into two logistically separate units (although financially they remained one and the same). The Red Room houses magazines which display both nudity and explicit sexual acts in progress. There are also a great many novels whose covers and advertisements (on the covers or the fly-leaves) promise sexual sensationalism. A sign on the wall reads: "Soiled or damaged merchandise must be paid for." The room is brightly lit, is uncarpeted, and contains only the books, magazines, and shelves and cases with which to display them.

The Brown Room houses novels and poems by recognized literary figures from the past 6 centuries, including Chaucer, Rabelais, Balzac, Twain, Lawrence, and Joyce. A sign reads: "Every book in this room was written by a great master and deals with sex and erotica in a straightforward manner." There is also a section of art books and art photography books, the relevant sign reading, "This is how the masters saw it and see it—the naked body." The room is carpeted, mildly lit, and has several easy chairs for the customers.

The Society for the Prevention of Intellectual Trash (S.P.I.T.) and the Committee for Combatting the Curse of Pornography (C.C.C.P.) have started a campaign to rid Fair City of all such material. They bring Smutte to court.

Choosing whichever side you wish to represent, make a thorough argument why the store should or should not be allowed to continue operation. You may wish to argue how the store might be modified in order to continue its operation (if you are arguing against Smutte).

✝